STORIES FROM A LIFE

STORIES FROM A LIFE

TRUSTING GOD

Brett Ray

But I am like an olive tree

flourishing in the house of God;

I trust in God's unfailing love

for ever and ever .

—King David

Psalm 52:8 (NIV)

Scripture taken from the HOLY BIBLE, NEW INTERNATIONAL VERSION®. NIV®. Copyright© 1973, 1978, 1984 by International Bible Society. Used by permission of Zondervan. All rights reserved.

ISBN 1-59971-289-X

Cover Design: Gordon Henderson
Photography: Leigh Anne Page
Art: Kelly Ray

Right Choice Communications
P.O. Box 321
Holly, MI 48442
www.BrettRay.com

CONTENTS

TO CAROL
MY BESTEST FRIEND

AND TO STEVE BOURQUE
EVEN THE LOSERS GET LUCKY SOMETIMES

ACKNOWLEDGMENTS

Thank you to my editor, Heather Gemmen for doing what you do so well.

Special thanks to:

Gordon and Kim Henderson for your friendship and guidance along the way.

Mary Hyde for your treasured friendship to Carol and an extra set of eyes for me.

Leigh Anne Page for your wonderful encouragement and for being the best business manager and friend a family could hope for. I am so grateful.

My incredible prayer team: Leslie Betts, Steve Bourque, Kristy Endersby, Kristen Hartsell, Jen and Russ Kacin, Greg and Autumn Lineberger, Greg and Sandy McDonough, Kristina McVety, Tom and Julia Phillips, Kaley Page, Leigh Anne Page, Eileen VanZee, Madison Withrow and Julie White – I am never alone.

Jerry and Charlotte Martin for living and breathing the Gospel.

John Mathers for being a wonderful friend who keeps pushing me outside my comfort zone.

John Waters for being there all through the years.

Gary and Sharon Page, Mike and Diane Hennessy, O'Brien and Denise Robertson - We want to be like you when we grow up.

Gary Stanley for your friendship and inspiration.

Tim Downs for your advice and wisdom.

Mom and Dad for all your loving support.

ACKNOWLEDGMENTS

Steve Bourque - Thanks for using your gifts in my life to love and teach me.

Josh, Stephen, Andrew, Kelly and Mareah for being my best friends.

Carol - Sometimes I think God's favorite way to spoil me is through you. You are the one I love.

And to my King, the Lord Jesus Christ. You are the same yesterday, today and forever and your grace means everything to me.

INTRODUCTION

To trust in him when no need is pressing,
when things seem going right of themselves,
may be harder than when things seem going wrong.
—George MacDonald

I used to think that trusting God meant leaning on him during the difficult times in my life. However, over the last several years, God has been showing me that he wants me to trust him through the trials, yes, but also with every area of my life. He wants me to trust him every day with my family and friends, with my fears and failures. He even wants me to trust him with my sin and doubt. This book is a collection of true short stories from my life, which shows my journey on the path to trusting God with all that I am and all that I have.

—Brett Ray

Chapter One

GOODBYE PARADISE

Sin

Is it just me, or somewhere deep down inside, do you feel that God is going to deal you a bad hand? Doesn't each one of us wonder at times if God is going to give up on us? Maybe he will finally say, "Alright, that's it. I've had enough—enough of your sin, enough of your failure, enough of you. I'm done."

It's certainly something I've feared. And this fear was driven by my Sunday school knowledge of God's behavior.

In the Begining

The very first time that humans ever blew it was all the way back in the Garden of Eden, in paradise. God placed the man and the woman in a perfect world. In the middle of the garden stood two unique trees: the tree of life—which when eaten from would allow you to live forever (Genesis 3:22)—and the tree of the knowledge of good and evil—which when eaten from would allow you to be like God, knowing good from evil (Genesis 3:22). God joyfully gave them the tree of life to eat from—as much as they wanted and whenever they wanted. However, he commanded them not to eat from the tree of the knowledge of good and evil.

So what did they do? They ate from the tree of knowledge of good and evil. They took the forbidden fruit and dove in. They sinned. They disobeyed God. They blew it. They separated themselves by their sin from a perfect God.

What was God's response?

First, he called them naked. That's not very nice.

Second, he punished them. I don't like that one.

Third, he kicked them out. No wonder I'm feeling a little insecure.

He called them names, he cursed them, and he kicked them out. If that's how he deals with sin, how can I trust God?

I'm not a little boy anymore, and my understanding of Scripture needs to be accurate. I'm ready to pick apart each of these three reactions and try to better understand God's purposes.

Naked

Nakedness evokes intense emotion. I remember the first time I ever realized I was naked. When I was three years old, my parents grew sunflowers in our backyard. One morning I woke up, did my business in the bathroom, and ran outside to look up at these giant plants that seemed to touch the sky. I saw a neighbor over the fence, and I shared my enthusiasm with her: "Look at our sunflowers!"

She didn't look at the flowers though. Instead she said, "Look at you, young man. You need to go into the house and get some clothes on." I looked down, and to my horror, I realized that I was standing naked in front of this woman. I turned and ran into the house as fast as my little legs would carry me, crying to my mother to rescue me.

Being naked is being vulnerable. I was speaking at a summer camp, years ago, in Michigan. On one of the hot afternoons, we loaded up the buses and took the kids to the lake. The dunes near Silver Lake are huge, and before the kids hit the water, they exhausted themselves climbing up these giant sandy landscapes and then rolling or running down them. Some people were using plastic sleds to race down the steep sides of the dunes. The hill closest to the lake—notoriously named "The Cliff"—was too high and too steep to run or sled down.

Eventually we gave up the hills for the waves. The beach was packed. People were everywhere, in and out of the water. As we were tossing Frisbees, a man stood at the top of The Cliff, sand sled in hand, and let out a war cry—letting us all know he was going to attempt to slide down the giant hill, taking his life into his own hands. Everyone stopped. He was a lunatic—and our hero at the same time. The man ran and leapt onto his sled. With lightning speed, he soared vertically to the water's edge where he splashed down and disappeared under the surface. We all held our breath. Suddenly he burst out, fists in the air, alive and victorious. The crowd went nuts.

Before we could settle down, his companion stood at the top of The Cliff and waved her sand carpet in the air in preparation for her own descent. If we thought he went down fast, we knew she would go even faster. She weighed about twice as much as he did and looked very determined not to be outdone. The beach audience stood rapt. She leapt. She achieved incredible speed— going so fast that she didn't realize that her sled went *zip* from underneath her and her bathing suit went *zip* from underneath her. With a great splash, she disappeared under the surface of the water. Seconds later, she burst out of the water with a look of sincere accomplishment on her face.

Everyone exploded with laughter, pointing at her. Her expression of victory turned to shame. I could see a scar being written across her heart that would never be erased. The crowd continued howling; people doubled over, saying or gesturing one message: "You're naked, lady, in front of a whole beach full of people. You're naked!" Her companion ran up the sand to grab her suit—but the damage was already done.

That night, back at camp, I was angry. "Why did you have to laugh?" I asked the students. I had been in her position too many times in my past to let them get away with that. Not physically naked, but emotionally naked. I know what it is like to endure people pointing and laughing at my vulnerability. Nakedness is powerful.

God called Adam and Eve "naked." Right? Doesn't the Bible say that God got right in their faces, laughed, pointed out their sin, and called them naked? That's what I always thought. But if you look closer in Genesis chapter three, you see that after Adam and Eve ate from the forbidden tree, they were afraid. When they heard God walking in the garden, they hid themselves. When God called after them and asked where they were Adam replied, "I heard you in the garden, and I was afraid because I was naked; so I hid."

God then said, "Who told you that you were naked? Have you eaten from the tree that I commanded you not to eat from?" (Genesis 3:8-11).

God never called them naked. He didn't shame them at all. Rather, he covered their shame. God dressed Adam and Eve. He shed the blood of an innocent animal, made garments of skin, and clothed them (Genesis 3:21). He covered them. He loved them.

Does this sound familiar? The blood of an innocent man, who was called the Lamb of God, was shed to cover our shame. Jesus Christ died on the cross to replace our disgrace with salvation. According to God's purpose, the One who was without sin took on our sin. Whether Jesus was naked on the cross or allowed a covering to hide his circumcision, he was painfully exposed so our sins could be covered.

Now, that's got my attention, and it's a little different from what I grew up thinking.

Punished

Perhaps he didn't shame us, but can we dodge the punishment part so easily? Think back to the Garden of Eden story: after they sinned, God handed out the penalties. To the woman he said, "I will greatly increase your pains in childbearing; with pain you will give birth to children. Your desire will be for your husband and he will rule over you." To Adam he said, "Because you listened to your wife and ate from the tree about which I commanded you, 'You must not eat of it,' cursed is the ground because of you; through painful toil you will eat of it all the days of your life. It will produce thorns and thistles for you, and you will eat the plants of the field. By the sweat of your brow you will eat your food until you return to the ground, since from it you were taken; for dust you are and to dust you will return" (Genesis 3:16-19).

So what God was saying was, "Eve, giving birth is going to be a painful experience and your husband will rule over you. Adam, your work is now going to be costly. You're going to have to sweat it out and then you will die."

That's some heavy-duty punishment.

But suppose I am looking at this wrong. Perhaps God didn't punish Adam and Eve that day in the garden. Perhaps he merely disciplined them. You may be thinking, "Punishment, discipline, same thing." No. Big difference. Punishment has everything to do with shame. Discipline has everything to do with love. Let me give you some examples.

My daughter spills her milk all over the table and all over her plate, ruining her dinner. Suppose I say to her, "What are you, some kind of idiot? You're big enough to know better than to do something stupid like that. I'm not cleaning up after your mess. Clean it up yourself. Why don't you learn to use your brains once in awhile?" Now, is that punishment or discipline? It's all about shaming her, humiliating her. It's punishment.

Let me give you a different example. A true story this time. From time to time, I will take one of the kids with me on a business trip. My kids often call me Papa, so we call it "Papa Time." Years ago, when he was little, I took my oldest son, Joshua, on a weekend retreat with me. We walked into the hotel and up to the counter where we needed to check in. I turned to Joshua and said, "Stand right here next to me and don't leave Papa's side." I started to check in.

A moment later I glanced down at Josh. He was gone. My heart froze. I looked to my right and left. No Josh. In a panic, I turned to the woman behind the counter and asked, "Did you see where my son went?" She shook her head no. I looked down the hall to my left—no Josh. Then to my right—he was not there. I turned around and looked behind me.

There he was, standing by the pool with a very excited look on his face. "Papa," he said when he saw me, "they have a pool!"

"Joshua"—my voice sounded calmer than I felt—"come here. You are in trouble."

He walked up to me and asked, "Why?"

"I would like for you to tell me why."

"Because you told me to stand next to you and not go anywhere and I walked away?"

I said, "That's right. Now, when we get up to our room I am going to discipline you, and then we will have the fun I've planned for us. Stand here next to me and don't go anywhere." I looked back up to the desk and said, "Sorry about that." I went back to checking in.

I glanced down a minute later and Josh was gone. I didn't panic. I turned toward the pool and there was Josh. I signaled for him to come back to me and told him he was in bigger trouble now.

He asked, "Why?"

"You tell me."

"Because two times you told me to stand next to you and I didn't listen?"

"That's right."

When we got to our room, the first thing I did was to lovingly discipline Joshua. When his discipline was over, guess what he did. He leapt into my arms, tears running down his cheeks, and wrapped his arms around my neck. Why? Because discipline has everything to do with love. I held him and told him I loved him. I disciplined him because I love him more than life itself, and I would rather do that than have him end up at the bottom of the pool.

My daughter Kelly was getting ready once to put her fingers into a fan. I gently slapped her hand and said, "No, no, Kelly. Don't touch." Of course she didn't like her hand being slapped and she cried. Better for her to be disciplined than to lose her fingers.

What makes me think Adam and Eve were disciplined in the Garden and not punished? The simple truth is that they could not have handled the punishment for their sins. The punishment for their sins was eternal separation from God. The wages or cost of sin is death (Romans 6:23). However, even as God named that consequence, he promised that freedom for his children would come (Genesis 3:15). The punishment for their sin was taken on by Jesus at the cross.

If you are a child of God, you will not be punished for your sins. Jesus Christ was humiliated, shamed, and punished once and for all. In other words, you don't need to be punished. God sent his Son to pay the price, cost, or wages for your sin. He who was without sin became despised and cursed. He died in your place so you don't have to be eternally separated from God. Then he victoriously rose from the dead.

God doesn't punish those who repent; he disciplines. Even as he recited the consequences Adam and Eve created for themselves, he gave them the biggest hug that was ever given. I don't know if he did it physically, but he did it verbally. This is what he said to the serpent, to the evil one who led Adam and Eve astray: "The offspring of the woman will crush his head and you will strike his heel" (Genesis 3:15). The offspring of the woman is Jesus. The hug is God's promise that Jesus will crush Satan's head by dying on the cross. However, this cost Jesus dearly. The cost is that Jesus' foot coming down on Satan's head will be pierced (and not only were his feet pierced, but his hands and side as well) and then he would die. The first time the cross of Jesus is mentioned is in the book of Genesis. Right from the beginning God had a plan to rescue Adam and Eve from their sin.

People punish people, people punish themselves, but God never punishes his children. The New Testament speaks frequently about how those who reject Jesus Christ will be punished; but only once in the New International Version of the New Testament is the word *punishment* used in referring to God's people, and this verse is speaking of how God lovingly disciplines his children (Hebrews 12:6). God's purpose was that Jesus would take our punishment once and for all, so we could be lovingly disciplined and forgiven.

Kicked Out

He didn't call us naked. He covered our shame.

He didn't punish us. He gave our punishment to Jesus Christ.

But that doesn't take care of the biggest fear this little boy inside of me had—that God was going to get fed up with me and kick me out.

Remember the tree of life in the Garden? What made it so wonderful is that whoever ate from it would live forever. Adam and Eve were allowed to eat the fruit any time they wanted—until now. God no longer wanted them to eat from the tree of life because if they did, they would be stuck with their sin forever. Adam and Eve needed to die physically so they could rise again by the power of God, born again spiritually into their new perfect bodies. The Garden of Eden with its tantalizing tree was the most dangerous place on the planet for them. God loved Adam and Eve too much to allow them to eat from this fruit, so he removed them from the Garden. He banished them from the danger and put a spiritual guard to block the entrance so they could never return. "So the Lord God banished him from the Garden of Eden to work the ground from which he had been taken. After he drove the man out, he placed on the east side of the Garden of Eden cherubim and a flaming sword flashing back and forth to guard the way to the tree of life" (Genesis 3:23-24).

When I was in college, one of my classmates told a story about when he was a lifeguard, years before. Even though it was a beautiful day, he was instructed to get all of the kids out of the pool because of a thunderstorm that was quickly moving in. He blew his whistle and yelled for all of the kids to get out of the pool. One little boy stood defiant in the pool refusing to get out.

"It's not safe," the lifeguard warned. "Get out of the pool or I will come in and take you out myself."

"I'm not getting out," the boy replied.

While the lifeguard was getting ready to go in to get this rebellious little boy, lightning struck the pool. People were knocked down from the powerful blast. When the lifeguard looked up, he saw the boy floating dead in the pool.

Just as the lifeguard was trying to save the boy's life by banishing him from the pool, so God banished Adam and Eve from the garden to save their lives. God is still rescuing people every day from eternal death. Because we are born spiritually dead we must become born again in Christ so we can live forever. God's purpose is to keep us from eternal separation from him so we can live forever with Christ.

When God looks at me he sees a brand new child, forgiven because of what Jesus has done for me through the cross and his resurrection. It has helped me so much to realize that my identity is not in my sin, but rather in the person of Jesus Christ. This has changed my life in many ways. Now I go before the throne of God a child saved by grace rather than a sinner sentenced to death. I am forgiven and have been made brand new in Christ.

Forgiven

This story of Adam and Eve is taken from the first book of the Bible. The last chapter of the last book of the Bible tells us that those of us who are in heaven will once again see the fruit from the tree of life, planted next to the river of life (Revelation 22:1-2). And we will have the right to the tree of life (Revelation 22:14).

As his children we can trust God with our lives. He has made the way for us to be forgiven and accepted. He has covered our shame. He disciplines us because he loves us. He will never kick us out; he will never give up on us. Ever.

Chapter Two

BEYOND A SHADOW

Doubt

Not everyone believes in miracles. I, however, not only believe in them, I have witnessed them.

Hard to Believe

My oldest son, Joshua, has always had a childlike faith. Since he was young, he has believed in miracles, believed in God, and believed in God's love for him. He recently started Junior High, but has not lost that simple faith. However, I remember the first time I saw doubt in his eyes, when he was still young.

I sat down to prepare for our weekly family Bible study. I would often peek ahead at the passage I would be reading to see if I needed any props in telling the story. For example, one day we read about the Israelites, God's chosen people. They had complained to God because they had no food in the wilderness. God provided manna, a thin flaky bread that the people found on the ground when they woke up in the morning. To illustrate manna, Carol and I took pita bread, tore it up into pieces, and put it in our pockets. After we read the story, the kids prayed; while their eyes were closed, we threw the pita bread all over the floor. When they opened their eyes they cried, "What is it?"

"It's manna," we explained. Manna means, "What is it?"

Before I got started on this lesson, Carol came to me and said, "That pound of hamburger we just fried up for dinner was our last."

"We're out of hamburger?"

"Honey, we're out of food."

I asked her how our bank account looked.

"As empty as our refrigerator. But let's not worry about it. God will provide for us."

I went back to preparing for our family devotions. I opened the Children's Bible to take a peek at that evening's story. To my surprise, I read about someone who had also run out of food: the prophet Elijah. God performed an incredible miracle for him. I called Carol over and said, "Look at this story. This will make a great object lesson for all of us." I called the kids into the kitchen and announced that we were going to start our Bible reading (we call it "Circle Time").

Joshua said, "We have Circle Time in the family room, not in the kitchen."

"Tonight we start in the kitchen. Now, someone open up the refrigerator and tell me what we're going to have for breakfast tomorrow."

Josh stepped forward and opened the fridge. "Ummm...ketchup?" he asked. "Let me check the freezer," he suggested. "Lift me up," he said, so I did. "It's empty, too!" he exclaimed. He ran over to the pantry with his little siblings following him. The pantry—usually full of items like tuna, mac-n-cheese, chips, peanuts, and snacks—was empty.

Josh spun around. "We need to go to the bank," he declared.

"There's no money in there, Josh," I said quietly.

Josh nervously replied, "Well, then, we need to go to the magic wall."

Carol and I looked at each other in confusion.

"You know, the magic wall," he said. "You put your card in and the money comes out."

Carol and I laughed and said, "There's no money in the magic wall."

Joshua burst into tears. "We're going to starve!"

We hadn't expected such a strong reaction, and we both reached out to comfort him. I explained to him that I thought we should settle down, read our Bible story, and then decide if we were going to starve.

I read the miracle story about God bringing food, delivered by birds, to Elijah. I shut the Bible and said, "So, Josh, what do you think about that?"—and that is when I saw the doubt in his eyes.

"Papa," he said, "God does not always choose to do miracles." Josh has always been a little bit of an intellectual.

I lifted my eyebrows and said, "You're right, Josh. God does not always choose to do miracles. However, I do believe he will provide for his people. Mom and I are not doubting God on this one. It's up to you; what will you believe?"

Josh thought about it and said, "Well, if you and Momma are going to believe, then I'm going to believe."

I explained to Josh that he could not borrow his mother's faith or mine. It had to be his own. Josh told us that he was going to believe. We put the kids to bed and I went to meet with the group of guys I hang out with on Monday nights.

After spending some time catching up with the guys, I went out to my van and opened the door. My van was packed full of groceries. I stood there with my mouth hanging open. I closed the door and went back into the house. I asked the guys who put the groceries in my van. One of them said, "I did."

"Why?" I asked, amazed.

"I don't know; we had extra."

"John, how long have we been meeting now on Monday nights?"

"Maybe ten years. Why?"

"And over those years, you have never packed my van full of groceries."

"I don't usually have extra," John said, laughing.

I hadn't talked about my financial concerns with my friends, but now I couldn't stay quiet. I told my friends the story about the last pound of hamburger and Elijah's bird miracle and Joshua's doubt. Now it was their turn to be astonished. Could all of this have been a great coincidence? I don't think so. It was a miracle.

I went home that night and woke Joshua. He came downstairs and watched me unpack the groceries. He learned an important lesson: God is bigger than his doubt. For months after that, whenever we would pray (at dinner, bedtime, before school), Josh would say at the end of his prayers, "Oh, and God, thank you for our food miracle."

We're in Good Company

Who was the greatest doubter in the Bible? Some might say the disciple Peter. Even though he was a committed follower, he denied he knew Jesus. Some might say Moses. He came up with excuse after excuse not to go on the mission God had in store for him. And of course there's Thomas, from whom we get the term *Doubting Thomas.* The other disciples said that Jesus had risen from the dead and they had seen him, but Thomas said, "I won't believe until I see him for myself." Even Jesus' mother and brothers came to take charge of him at one point because they thought he was mad.

Doubt can be found in the eyes of God's followers throughout the Scriptures. But perhaps the greatest doubter in the Bible is the man whom Jesus named one of the greatest men of all time (Matthew 11:11). A relative of Jesus, a great hero of the Bible: John the Baptist.

If anyone should not have doubted Jesus, it was John. John's purpose in life was to prepare the way for Jesus. The prophet Isaiah predicted the coming of John the Baptist years before he was born.

It is written in Isaiah the prophet:

"I will send my messenger ahead of you,

who will prepare your way"—

"a voice of one calling in the desert,

'Prepare the way for the Lord,

make straight paths for him.'" (Mark 1:2-3).

When he was a newborn, John's father prophesied about John: "You will go on before the Lord to prepare the way for him..." (Luke 1:76).

STORIES FROM A LIFE 23

When John started his ministry, his message was that he was not the Christ, but the one who would prepare the way for Jesus to come (John 1:19-28).

When John saw Jesus coming toward him he proclaimed, "Look, the Lamb of God, who takes away the sin of the world!" (John 1:29).

God told John that the one he saw the Spirit land on was the Son of God (John 1:32-34). When John baptized Jesus, he saw the Holy Spirit descend on Jesus as a dove. Then he heard a voice from Heaven proclaim: "This is my Son, whom I love; with him I am well pleased" (Matthew 3:17). John had the Trinity with him in that moment. He could touch the Son, see the Spirit, and hear the Father.

Wouldn't you think if there were anyone in the history of the world who should not doubt Jesus, it would be John?

However, after the baptism of Jesus, Herod had John thrown into prison. On Herod's birthday, Herod agreed to have John beheaded (Matthew 14:3-12). From prison, possibly now in his darkest hour, John sends Jesus a message. The message did not say, "Hey, Jesus, it was great being a part of this whole thing with you. Looks like it could be the end for me but that's okay. I believe in you and I know I will see you in heaven one day. Best wishes, your cousin, John." It also did not say, "Jesus, I'm a little afraid here, but now's not the time to lose faith. Say a few prayers for me. Love, John."

This is what the message was: "Are you the One who was to come, or should we expect someone else?" (Matthew 11:2-3).

John doubted.

But God was bigger than John's doubt. Jesus responded in the best way possible: "Go back and report to John what you hear and see: The blind receive sight, the lame walk, those who have leprosy are cured, the deaf hear, the dead are raised, and the good news is preached to the poor. Blessed is the man who does not fall away on account of me" (Matthew 11:4-6). He didn't chastise, he didn't push to convince, he didn't give up on John; he simply sent people to give witness to what he was doing. It was as if Jesus was gently saying to John, "I'm right here, John, it's me."

Moving Beyond Doubt

It brings me comfort to know that a man like John the Baptist could doubt. There's hope for me. Jesus could handle John's doubt so he can handle my doubt. Jesus' loving response when I doubt is, "I'm right here Brett. It's me. I'll keep doing what I do as you move beyond your doubt into faith."

I don't know if you're doubting. I don't know if you are worried or afraid. If you are, Jesus Christ can move you beyond your doubt. He's alive and he wants you to believe. Maybe it's belief itself you doubt. Ask him to help you see with his eyes. He can give you a childlike faith. He'll show you that he still heals broken hearts and broken lives, he still moves people beyond doubt and into belief in him, and he is still in the business of doing miracles.

One December morning I was sitting in my office at home when Carol came in. She explained to me that this December was going to be different for her: she had determined not to get stressed out. For years my speaking schedule has slowed down in the month of December—which is great for my family life, but bad for our finances. "Every year around this time I manage to ruin the holidays by worrying and doubting," she told me. "But every year God shows up and does some miracle. We always have a wonderful Christmas and the bills all get paid. This year," she resolved, "I will not worry or doubt. I will enjoy this time in faith."

I told her I was very proud of her. She asked me if I would pray with her, so we knelt down and committed our needs into God's hands. "Father," Carol began, "I want to trust you this season with our finances—"

"How much?" I interrupted.

"How much what?" Carol asked.

"How much are we short? I know you have a number in your head."

"God knows how much we're short this month."

"I know God knows, but *I* want to know. I think God likes it when we pray specifically."

"Well, with Christmas, the bills, and the move into our new house, we're short $4,000."

"Okay." And we went back to praying.

That night before bed, we prayed again.

The next day someone knocked at our door. I peeked out the window and stared into the face of an old friend I had not seen for awhile. I opened the door and excitedly said, "What are you doing here?"

"It's Christmastime, and I had to come by and say hi to the Rays." He gave me a big hug and slipped something into my back pocket. I had him sit down in the family room while I went into the kitchen to get him something to drink—and, of course, to find out what was in my back pocket. What did I find there? A check. How much was the check for? Four thousand dollars! Not a penny more, not a penny less. I stumbled out into the family room and handed him his soft drink. I stuck the check in his face and asked, "What's this?"

He smiled and said, "That's just a little Christmas present for the Rays."

"No, really. What is this? We haven't told anyone."

He asked, "Told anyone what?"

"Just tell me how this came about."

"Okay. The other night my wife and I were sitting at the dinner table and she said, 'I want to give the Rays three thousand dollars for Christmas.' I looked at her and said, 'I don't know why, but it's supposed to be four thousand.' She said, 'Great. Write the check.'"

This could have been a coincidence. I don't think it was. God is still in the business of doing miracles. God does not always choose to do miracles, but he always wants to move us beyond doubt and worry into a world of faith and belief.

My favorite verse in the Bible is Hebrews 13:8: "Jesus Christ is the same yesterday and today and forever." He never changes. He never will change. We can trust him. We can let go of our doubt and put it into his hands because he is big enough to handle our doubt.

As I write this, December is a month away. It doesn't matter if we have money this year to buy the kids gifts for Christmas. What does matter is that the Ray family understands that the Jesus whose birth we celebrate on Christmas day is the same Jesus who will spend this Christmas with his cousin John the Baptist, Thomas, Peter and any other doubters who will look in his eyes and say, "I believe."

Chapter Three

LULLABIES AND PRAYERS

Testimonies

I love to listen to stories, and ever since I was a kid I have loved to tell stories. In this chapter I want to simply share a few stories about my family. They are stories of saving grace and simple, childlike faith. Children are amazing. They believe. If you tell them there is a God who is alive and who loves them, they believe. My children received God's grace into their lives when they were young, with very little help from my wife or myself. It was God who opened their eyes.

Joshua

When our oldest son, Joshua, was to be dedicated at church, our pastor encouraged us to pick a theme Bible verse for his life. He told us to try to find a creative way to teach Josh his verse so he wouldn't forget it. I decided to write a lullaby using the verse, and to sing it to him at bedtime every night. I wrote out lyrics from the Bible verses, then I asked a musician friend of mine to write the melody. I sang the song to Josh, for the first time, on the day he was dedicated.

"Joshua, be strong and courageous. Lead the people to the nation I have promised Abraham. Joshua, be careful to obey me. To the right or to the left please don't ever turn away. And you know that I will bless you. I will bless you every day."

I did the same thing for Stephen and Andrew.

On the morning of Kelly's dedication, Carol rolled over in bed and said, "Let me hear it."

"Hear what?"

"Kelly's song. Don't tell me you forgot your daughter's dedication song."

I had forgotten. I grabbed the Bible and looked up the verses that Carol had picked out for Kelly. I started scribbling out lyrics and, without the help of my musician friends, stole who knows whose melody to go with it.

I needed somebody to critique the lullaby. Joshua has always been analytical and honest, so I called him upstairs. I told him that I had just written Kelly's new song and that I wanted him to tell me what he thought.

"Kelly gets a song like me and the brothers?"

"Yes," I said. "Now listen." I sang Kelly's lullaby.

Josh said, "It's good. However,"—I knew he would give me an honest opinion—"two times in the song you say, 'Give your life to him.' Who's *him*?"

"Who do you think 'him' is?"

He thought about it for a minute and then he said, "Me?"

"Nope, it's not you. Guess again."

"Oh, I know. It's Jesus."

"That's right. How did you know?"

"Because you and Momma gave your life to Jesus and now—" he paused, and with a questioning look on his face said, "You want Kelly to give her life to Jesus?"

I told him I prayed all the time that someday all of my children would have a personal relationship with Jesus. With a quizzical look on his face he said, "Okay. See ya." And he walked out of the room.

I didn't think much of it. Little did I know that he was standing in the hall, just outside my door. I went back to working on the song. A minute later Josh stuck his head into the bedroom and said, "Papa, do you think someday I could give my life to Jesus?"

"Absolutely."

"Okay," he said, and disappeared.

I went back to work. A minute later he stuck his head through the doorway and said, "Papa, do you think I could maybe give my life to Jesus today?"

I hesitated. I thought to myself that he was pretty young to make such a big decision. "Well, we'll see."

Again he said "Okay" and took a step backward into the hall.

I went back to writing. I know now that as he stood there, alone in the hall, God was doing something in his heart. A minute later, he stepped into the bedroom and said, "Papa?"

A little annoyed at being interrupted again I said,

"What, Josh?"

"Do you think I could give my life to Jesus right now?"

God's Spirit whispered to my heart and said, "Brett, stop doing what you're doing and pay attention to what I'm doing."

I told Josh to come over and sit on the bed next to me. I set the lullaby aside and asked Josh why he felt like he needed to give his life to Jesus. With a simple, childlike faith he said, "Papa, don't you know that if I died today and went to heaven, I wouldn't get in because of my sin? I need to give my life to Jesus."

Surprised, I asked, "Who taught you about sin?"

"Momma did."

I bet she did, I thought. Then I got serious. I explained as simply as I could how our sin separates us from God, that Jesus died on the cross in our place for all the bad things we had done, and that he rose from the dead so that we could have a relationship with God. Joshua was listening very intently to every word I was saying. "We get to heaven because of what Jesus did for us," I told him.

"I want a friendship with Jesus, Papa."

"You can. It's as simple as inviting him to come into your life. Once Jesus opens your eyes, your sins can be forgiven."

People try to complicate salvation and Christianity all the time, but it is simple enough for a child to understand. Jesus said in the book of Matthew that unless we change and become like little children, we will never enter the Kingdom of Heaven. What's so important about little children? They believe. That's why it's called a "childlike faith."

With tears in my eyes, I bowed my head with Josh. I helped him pray a simple little prayer. I watched my son surrender his life, to let go and give it to God. That day in church, Josh seemed to be telling everyone about his new friendship with Jesus. He has not stopped talking about Jesus ever since.

He even shared this divine friendship with a bully who hated him. This mean kid punched Josh almost every day for no reason. He got suspended from school for threatening to kill a teacher. You get the picture. Josh decided that instead of hating this kid, he would pray for him. One afternoon Josh sat next to the bully on the bus ride home. Josh asked him if he had spent any time thinking about what happens to you when you die.

"Why should I?" the bully responded.

"It's the most important thing anyone can think about!" Josh replied. Josh talked about heaven and hell and the price Jesus paid to make the way into heaven—and then gave the plan of salvation the Bible teaches.

"I thought the way you get into heaven was from being good."

Wow, kid, if that's what you think, you're not doing a very good job! Josh thought. Out loud, he explained that only God was perfect and that to get to God you had to know his Son. This boy seemed very interested in what Joshua was sharing, but they had come to his bus stop. Josh asked, "Would you like to talk more about this tomorrow on the way home?"

"Yes, I would," the kid said.

The next day on the ride home, Josh talked to him a little more and then just came out and asked him: "Would you like to invite Jesus Christ into your life?"

"Yes, I would."

They bowed their heads and Josh prayed a simple prayer. Josh continues today to pray for this boy and we have seen some incredible changes in his life.

Stephen and Andrew

Stephen and Andrew are our identical twin sons, a year younger than Joshua. Similar in more than just appearance, they are hard to tell apart. We get them mixed up on a daily basis. When they are sideways, back ways, or at a distance, it's very difficult to tell them apart. You have to look at them straight in the face, and sometimes even that doesn't work. We just call them "The Brothers," usually the "Brothers of Thunder." As much alike as they are, they are unique individuals. Stephen is a nut and keeps us laughing. Andrew is sensitive and compassionate.

About a year and a half after Kelly's dedication, our family was on the road for one of my speaking engagements. We got to the hotel room after I had spoken and the boys all ran up to me and asked me to tell them a story before they went to bed. I told them to get into their pajamas and I would tell them a story. After changing, they said, "We want to hear a true story."

"What kind of true story would you like to hear?"

"A scary true story."

I thought about it for a minute and while Carol was putting little Kelly to bed, I began. I told them the story of a little boy who was a good kid growing up. However, at about twelve years old, he started making really bad choices in his life. He began to steal, cheat, lie, and even get involved with drugs. He also began to run away from home, and one time as he was leaving, he broke his mother's fingers in the door as he slammed it shut. He didn't even care. His heart was hardened.

Three years went by with the boy living like this. The last time the boy ran away from home he stayed away for a long time—so long that he was kicked out of high school.

The boy was swimming in a lake one day when he got himself into a situation where he thought he might drown. While he was under the water he imagined God asking him this question, "Are you ready to see me face to face?" The boy knew the answer was no. He always believed in God, he just didn't want anything to do with God. He didn't drown that day. God helped him out of the lake. He sat down next to the water's edge and put his hand up in the air. He prayed a simple prayer to Jesus, "If you still want me God, I'm right here. Please forgive me for all my sins. Come into my life and be my God." The boy didn't see, hear or feel anything unusual until the next morning when he woke up. He felt forgiven. He felt brand new and Jesus has been his best friend ever since.

"Do you know who the boy was?"

With wide eyes, they said, "No."

"That messed-up boy who was given a second chance—he was me."

They were shocked. Though I had told that story many times in my life, and with much more detail, I had never told it to them.

They all chimed in, "You ran away from home?" "You got kicked out of school?" "You broke Grammy's fingers?"

"Yes," I told them. "But God saved me from all of that."

To my surprise, Joshua looked at Stephen and Andrew and said, "Okay, brothers, that is Papa's story—or his testimony. And as you may or may not know, I have a story of my own." He then began to tell his brothers the whole story about when he gave his life to Jesus on the day of Kelly's dedication. He told them all about Kelly's lullaby and praying with me in the bedroom.

He looked at Stephen and Andrew with a very serious look. He asked them right out, "Do you want a story of your own? Do you want to give your lives to Jesus, yes or no?"

Carol had finished putting Kelly to bed. She peeked around the corner and gave me a look that said, "Can you believe this? Is Joshua really leading Stephen and Andrew to Jesus?"

With great excitement, Stephen and Andrew looked back at Josh and said, "Yes! We want to give our lives to Jesus!"

Josh looked up at me and said, "Papa, I might need help with the prayer part."

You're doing just fine, buddy, I thought. But I prompted him, and Josh prayed a very simple prayer of confession, forgiveness, and acceptance of God's grace with his brothers. Like Josh, Stephen and Andrew have not stopped talking about Jesus ever since. They have let go of their lives and now belong to God.

Kelly

Two years younger than The Brothers is our daughter Kelly. Her majesty. Princess Buttercup. Actually, I call her my little half pint. She is kind-hearted and caring.

We were on our way home from church one day, pulling up into the driveway, when Kelly shouted out from the backseat, "I want to give my life to Jesus!" Carol and I looked at each other with the same look on our faces: "Here we go again."

"Okay, Kelly, let's go into the backyard," I said. We all sat down on the grass.

Kelly's a bit of a leader so she took charge. She said, "Okay, I want everyone to sit in a circle around me and put your hands on me." I'm not sure where she came up with that, but I kept myself from laughing out loud. Then she said, "I will also need someone to pray with me."

After confirming that Kelly understood about her sin, God's grace, and his forgiveness, I said, "Momma, why don't you pray with Kelly." We all bowed our heads and Jesus welcomed Kelly into the family of God. While we were praying, it gently began to rain. We were all getting wet and we didn't care. It was physically raining down on us, just as God's grace was raining down on my daughter.

Mareah

An eighteen-year-old girl died several years ago of stomach complications. We believe she died of starvation. Teenagers die like this every day in the country of Haiti. This girl left behind a one-year-old baby with no father in the picture. The girl's cousin, who was fifteen or sixteen, took the little baby into her care. However, she was nearly starving herself, and after three months realized that she could not take care of this little baby girl.

When she brought the baby into the mission's clinic, the baby was almost dead. The baby had stick arms, stick legs, a sunken face, protruding ribs, and a bloated stomach. Her body was scarred where bugs had been biting her. The baby was put into the hands of missionaries John and Beth McHoul, who slowly but surely saved the baby's life by nursing her back to health.

That little baby girl is our youngest daughter, Mareah. She is a miracle to us. Walking sunshine. Three years younger than Kelly, she is constantly smiling and people are drawn to her joyful spirit. You would never know today that she had once been starving. She is taller than 98% of the kids her age. She is a head taller than all of her friends. One of Carol's girlfriends said, "If Mareah gets any taller, you're going to have to tell her she was adopted"—which is kind of funny because Mareah is black and the rest of the family is white.

We foolishly thought that we had something to offer Mareah when we adopted her. Now we see that she is the one who had something to give to us with her joyful and loving spirit.

When Mareah asked Jesus to forgive her sins and come into her life, she was adopted for a second time. God the Father has adopted each one of our family members. "For he chose us in him before the creation of the world to be holy and blameless in his sight. In love he predestined us to be adopted as his sons through Jesus Christ, in accordance with his pleasure and will to the praise of his glorious grace, which he has freely given us in the One he loves" (Ephesians 1:4-6).

Carol

Carol's story is short and sweet. She was a good kid. She can remember getting into trouble twice while she was growing up—once for using her mother's razor in the bathtub as a little girl without permission, and once for accidentally writing a bad word on an eraser in the third grade. That's it! That's Carol's claim to shame. An eraser and a razor. She was a good pastor's kid who got good grades and had a good attitude about life.

It wasn't until she got to college that she got serious about her personal relationship with God. She realized that being good wasn't enough. She still needed God's grace to change her life. She was not so good that she could get into heaven on her own just as I was not so bad that I could outrun the grace of God. "For all have sinned and fall short of the glory of God" (Romans 3:23). We both needed God's perfect grace in our lives.

These are our stories—our testimonies of how we have let go of our lives and placed them into God's hands. God is writing new stories all the time. What is your story? Is Jesus Christ the God of your life? Have you confessed your sins to him? Have you been forgiven by his grace? Have you trusted him with your life? Have you let go of being your own god and allowed Jesus Christ to be in control, in charge, and Lord of your life?

He loves you, and he is just a simple prayer away.

Chapter Four

THE DYING OF SELF

Sacrifice

I had one week and I was sure I could do it. My Sunday school teacher challenged me to memorize a Bible verse, and I wanted the promised reward. The verse was John 15:13: "Greater love has no one than this, that he lay down his life for his friends."

Sunday came and I was ready. My teacher asked, "Now, did anyone—" My hand shot into the air. "Brett, do you know your memory verse?"

"Yes. Greaterlovehasnoonethanthisthatonelaydownhislifeforhisfriends John1513."

"That's great. Now what does it mean?"

What does it mean? She never said anything about understanding the verse, she just said memorize it.

"It doesn't help us to memorize the Bible if we don't know what it means," she urged.

I was trapped. I needed to come up with something and quick. I needed to explain when and where I would give up my life for my friends. "Someday when I grow up I'll be a missionary in Africa. My missionary friends and I will be tracking through the jungle when suddenly we will all be caught up in the net of a headhunter. He will say to us, 'I can kill all of you, or one of you can lay down his life to let the others go free.' At this point I will stick my hand out of the net and say, 'Okay, I memorized the verse. I knew it was coming someday when I would have to lay down my life for my friends. Cook me and let the others go free.'"

"Close enough," said my Sunday school teacher. She licked a star and put it on my forehead. (That was my reward. No wonder I hated Sunday school.)

Did you catch my interpretation of the verse? In some distant land, in some distant time, God would ask me to lay down my life. Not here. Not now. The truth is that God wants me to lay down my life today. God wants me to surrender now. It's tough. I probably resist dying to self as much as I resist physically dying.

Taco Bell Evangelism

I seemed to have had a better grasp of surrender when I first committed my life to Christ. After I put my life into God's hands, I went back home. Being back home was a little strange after running away, but I knew it was the right thing to do—and after all, I was only fifteen. I went back to school and talked to my teachers about letting me back into class. That was a little strange as well, after being kicked out. I also went back to church. I had grown up in church but was never interested in seeking out God, until now.

I remember my first night back at youth group. I went to a very large church and our youth group was really big. Before I would sit in the back and distract. This time, I was up front, wanting to learn more about my newfound friend and Lord, Jesus Christ. Someone had given me this little Bible that fit into my pocket and I had it out and was taking notes. Youth group had suddenly become very important to me and I grew to love it dearly.

After youth group, some older high school kids came up to me and said, "We understand you gave your life to Jesus."

"Yeah," I said. I was thinking, *Wow, this is cool. People have already heard about this.*

They said, "You want to go out for a bite to eat with us?"

Even cooler. They want to hang out with me. "Sure," I said casually. On the way to Taco Bell I kept thinking I really needed to watch my mouth and not let any cuss words slip out. I was a new Christian and I was not quite sure how to act, but I was pretty sure that cussing was probably not a good idea. We ordered our food and sat down.

Soon after that, the door flew open and in walked these college football players. They were not happy campers. I would find out later that they were "ex" players—they had been kicked off the team for suspicion of cocaine use. After ordering their food, they made a scene about where they were going to sit. Families were moving their children away from them and the manager glanced out from the kitchen, looking as if he was pondering calling the police. The athletes calmed down as they settled in with their food.

Have you ever accidentally made eye contact with someone? When this happens I always pretend like I am not looking at the person and slowly look away. I was eating and I looked up at the same time that one of these big, tough guys looked up at me. We locked eyes. I was getting ready to look down when something happened inside of me. I wasn't afraid, which was odd for me. I thought, *God lives inside of me and God's bigger than this guy.* I didn't look away; I just sat there and stared into those angry eyes. He glared back, a bit surprised to have a little punk like me staring him down. To my surprise, he shook his head and looked away as if to say, "You're not worth my time."

For the few seconds the stare down lasted, I had a couple of thoughts. First, this guy looked stoned. With the crowd I used to run with, I was very familiar with that glazed-over expression from being intoxicated or under the influence of something. Second, this guy probably didn't know God or trust him with his life.

Something welled up inside of me and I wanted to go over and tell him about my friendship with Jesus Christ. I looked over at my new friends from youth group and excitedly said, "Hey, guys, I think God wants me to talk to someone about him!"

"That's nice," they said. "Who is it?"

I pointed at the football players. "Those guys right over there."

They looked over at the Neanderthals eating their burritos and said, "Brett, God didn't tell you anything."

"What do you mean?"

With a slightly nervous edge to his voice, one of them said, "God doesn't work that way. He doesn't just tell people to talk to other people. We have been Christians for a long time, you have to trust us on this one."

"Look," I said, "I admit I don't know exactly how God works, but it seems to me that these guys might need to hear about God. Let's do it."

"No, Brett."

I was surprised, but not dissuaded. "All right, I'm going over with or without you." I guess I expected them to give in and join me. They didn't. I stood up.

"Brett, sit down."

I stepped away from the table and turned toward the football players. Time seemed to slow down. Things began to race through my mind as I slowly walked across the room. *I don't have a game plan. I have never done this before. God, what do I do?* Then I remembered a story from the Bible. God told Moses to speak to a hostile leader who was holding God's people hostage as slaves: The Pharaoh of Egypt. Moses told God no, and one of his excuses was that he didn't know what to say to Pharaoh. God told him, "You go, and I'll teach you what to say." I don't know how I remembered that story at that moment but I thought, *That's it, God will put the words into my mouth.*

I reached the football players and tapped one of them on the shoulder. He looked up at me with a glare. I opened my mouth and these are the words that came out: "Hey buddy, step outside." Instantly I was thinking, *All right God, I don't think I would have picked those words.*

I was ushered outside by these angry giants. They threw me up against a brick wall. One of them bent down, got in my face, and said, "What's up, punk?"

Okay God, I'm going to open my mouth again. Please come up with something better this time. "You're stoned, aren't you?" is what came out. Strike two.

He got closer to my face and said, "I have had a couple of beers, punk. What's it to you?"

"Alcohol isn't the answer to your problems. God is."

They threw me up against the wall again. "What, are you some kind of preacher? Are you going to preach at us?"

I started telling them all about God's kindness and about how he loved them. They took turns pushing and shoving me, but I didn't stop. I had decided that God had saved me from spending eternity in hell and I was going to allow him to do anything he wanted with my life. Webster's defines surrender as: "to give up or yield possession or power. The act of surrendering." I was willing to give up, or yield, to God's power and will for my life, no matter what the cost.

After a while, the football players settled down and were just asking me questions. I told them I didn't have all the answers, but I did have *the* answer: Jesus Christ. A couple of guys left and went back to the car, but two of them stayed: the guy I stared down and the guy I tapped on the shoulder. Before we parted ways, one of the guys looked me in the eye and said, "Brett, when I woke up this morning, I didn't believe there was a God, but now I do."

"Oh yeah; how's that?"

"Because obviously there's a God who's alive in you."

Motivation

I have changed a lot through the years. Most likely if I was in Taco Bell today under the same circumstances, I would get up and walk away. Why? Because back then I hadn't learned how to doubt God yet in my new life with him. These days, I too often let fear direct my path. Too often I close my eyes to the needs around me and say that someone else can take care of it. I'm praying that God will lead me back to the place of complete surrender to him, not just existence as a Christian.

I want to live my life so people can see there's something different about me—that God lives in me and through me. I want to surrender to him because he loves me, not so that he will love me. Too many times Christians have the wrong motivation for sharing their faith. They believe if they share their faith, God will be impressed and like them more. We can do nothing to make God like us any more than he already does. We share our faith because God loves us, not so that he will love us.

Recently, one of my sons told me he was feeling that he needed to spend more time with God.

"That's great," I told him, "but be sure that you're not trying to earn God's acceptance. I'm so proud of you that you read your Bible every morning before school—and that's something that will benefit you for a lifetime—but you should know that if you never opened your Bible again for the rest of your life, God would still love you the same." God loves it when we worship, read our Bibles, and share our faith. He wants us to do this out of a loving response to his grace, not to gain acceptance.

On the Plane

Being claustrophobic, I hate flying. However, I'm even more uncomfortable when I think God wants me to say something about him to the person sitting next to me. It's just easier to read and relax. Years ago, I had an extremely unusual flight. I was settled in, hoping that the empty seat beside me would stay that way—when the last passengers boarded. They were monsters. The letters on their matching jackets let me know they were world-renown wrestlers—the guys I've seen before on cable TV. They surrounded me. One very popular wrestler sat down right behind me. One sat down across the aisle, and—despite my prayers that some little elderly woman would magically appear next to me— one of these giants plunked in the empty seat beside me.

The plane took off. *Just eat your peanuts,* I told myself. *Look out the window, mind your own business, and nobody will get killed.* We began to experience some turbulence, and I glanced over at the guy sitting next to me to see if he was having any trouble with our rough and bumpy ride. I did a double take. Blood was dripping down his forehead and he didn't even realize it. The thought came to mind that I should tell him he was bleeding. *No, I* interrupted myself. *Just mind your own business. He's a big boy and can take care of himself.* The truth is, I was afraid to talk to this guy. I wrestled for a few minutes (no pun intended) with the idea of what to do, and couldn't find a good excuse not to do the right thing.

I swallowed hard and said, "Excuse me, sir. You're bleeding."

He looked over at me and said, "What did you say?"

I pointed to my forehead and said again,

"You're bleeding."

He reached his hand up and wiped his forehead. Seeing the blood on his palm he said, "Oh, thank you." He called the flight attendant, and she brought him some napkins and band-aids. I always thought wrestling on T.V. was completely fake until this man lifted up his hair, and I saw his scalp full of scars and stitches. One of his stitches must have popped out from the cabin pressure change during the turbulence.

He must have felt like he owed me some kind of explanation when he saw me staring with my mouth hanging open. Pointing to the guy sitting across the aisle, he said, "Hercules over there hit me over the head with a chair last night."

I didn't know how to respond so I just said, "Oh, yeah. I hate it when that happens."

He introduced himself. I shook his hand and said,

"I'm Brett."

"Brett, thanks for telling me I was bleeding."

"No big deal."

"Yes, it is. I appreciate it."

Little did he know how big of a deal it was.

"So, do you fly much?" he asked. I told him that I did and he said, "Yeah, me too." We then started making small talk about life on the road. While we were talking about hotels, airports, and living out of suitcases, I looked into his eyes and saw a lot of pain—and this kind of pain had nothing to do with chairs hitting him on the head. *Ask him what's wrong,* my heart prompted. I knew that this was one of those moment when God was asking me to let go of my will and my fears, and to trust him with the outcome.

I swallowed hard once again, and asked him if there was something wrong.

He got a serious look on his face, squinted a little bit and said, "Why do you ask?"

"I guess I ask because I care."

"You care? What do you mean, you care?"

I told him that I used to be a rebellious teenager and didn't care about anyone but myself. I shared with him my near-death experience that brought me to Christ. "And now I care about people I don't even know," I said. "I think God cares through me."

"Brett, I don't know who you are or where you came from, but I needed to hear that today."

"You needed to hear what?"

"That someone cares about me."

I sighed and said, "Tell me. What's going on?"

His eyes got wet. His lip started to quiver slightly as he said, "My baby daughter just died. I don't know what to do. I was able to go home for the funeral but now I'm back on the road and it will be the same thing tonight on the phone. My wife will be begging me to come home. I don't know what to do. I have a contract. I want to be home. I just don't know what to do. It's just nice to know that somebody on this stinking planet still cares about somebody else."

"I do care," I said. "But more importantly, God cares. He understands the pain in your heart and I don't." Then, before I knew what I was doing, I asked him if I could pray with him.

He looked me in the eyes and said, "I think I need that." We bowed our heads and I prayed for him. When we got off the plane, he took me by the shoulders and said, "I will never forget you."

"It's okay if you forget me," I said, "just don't forget Jesus. He loves you so much."

To think that I almost didn't say anything. I almost did what I usually do: stay in my comfort zone and mind my own business. All around us people are hurting, dying to be loved. God wants to touch these people; but he wants to use you and me to do it. Will we surrender? Will we die to ourselves so that God can do what he wants to in our lives?

Timing

My daughter Kelly just came into the room and asked if I could go outside and ride bikes with her. My first thought was, *I'm writing.* My second thought was, *My bike is already put away for the season.* I know. I need to go bike riding with Kelly. I know I'll enjoy it once I'm out there—it's just that getting the bike out is a bit of a hassle. And I'm doing something else right now, something important. I'm writing about Jesus.

You see, John 15:13 ("Greater love has no one than this, that he lay down his life for his friends") is really a verse about Jesus. He died for us, willingly gave his life to save ours. However, Jesus died to self every day before he physically died. Jesus died for us long before he died on the cross.

Will I let that life be my example? Will I take up my cross and follow him? Will I trust God and surrender my life each day? "God, I give up my life today to do what it is you want me to do. To sacrifice my personal space to spend time investing in my children one on one. To help my wife carry the load around the house by serving her and the kids. To fold laundry or make lunches or wash the dishes. To let her know that she really matters by asking her how her day was, and then listening. To ask the guy on the airplane sitting next to me, pouring out his heart, if there is anything I can pray for him about."

I really struggle with this area of my life. I want to do what I want to do, when I want to do it, but for now, I'm off to ride bikes with Kelly.

P.S. While we were riding bikes I asked Kelly what her favorite part of the day was. She said, "Papa, my favorite part of the day is right now."

Chapter Five

BROKEN BONES

Trials

A Bad Day

My cell phone rang. A nervous voice on the other end of the line said, "Mr. Ray, this is the secretary from the elementary school. There's been an accident."

No parent wants to hear those words. My heart sank, my stomach tied itself in a knot, and I started to feel queasy. The secretary said, "It's your daughter Kelly. You need to come right away."

I felt a chill run down my spine as I yelled to Carol that there had been an accident at the school and to keep the phone close. Hands trembling on the steering wheel, I made the short trip to school in what felt like hours. I pulled up to the curb, not knowing what to expect, and two adults were standing in the parking lot waiting for me. They escorted me into the office where a crowd surrounded my daughter. I turned the corner and there was little Kelly, her precious blood splattered on her outfit.

"She fell off the monkey bars…" someone told me. I barely heard the explanation. All I could absorb was what I saw in front of me. Kelly's arm was snapped completely in two. Her arm was bent in gruesome fashion and the bone had come all the way through her skin. Nobody was touching her. (I think everyone was afraid to.)

Kelly looked up and said, "Papa."

Her first-grade teacher was kneeling down next to her. When he saw me he said, with a nervous edge in his voice, "Mr. Ray, I am so glad you're here."

I wanted to sink to the ground, but I knew I couldn't. I needed to be steady for my frightened little girl. I went over and knelt down in front of Kelly. It seemed as though everyone got quiet, wondering what I would say.

"Kelly, we're going to get you put back together right away."

I gently scooped her up into my arms—and she let out a scream. I loaded her into the car and buckled her seat belt—and she let out another scream. Every time we went over a crack in the road on the way to the hospital, she screamed. I must say, though, that in between screams she had a very brave look on her face and she wasn't crying. My biggest concern at that moment was that she might pass out, so I thought I should keep her talking.

"Kelly, the most important thing to do right now is to talk to Papa."

"Okay," she said.

"How was your day?" I asked her. (What a great question to ask a child who has just broken her arm in two.)

She looked down at her arm dangling and said, "Okay."

And then I remembered that I needed to call Carol. I wanted to give the news carefully because I didn't want to scare Kelly by letting her know how horrible I thought her arm looked. I dialed.

"Hi, honey."

"What's going on?" Carol demanded.

"Kelly just had a little accident."

"Where are you now?"

In my nicest voice I replied, "Oh, we're on the way to the hospital."

"Brett, what's going on?"

"Okay," I said. "I'll talk to you later."

We pulled up to the emergency room and I carried Kelly in. The lady behind the counter started in an apathetic voice, "May I help—" Then she saw Kelly's arm and jumped out of her chair. She ran into the back room and started yelling orders. Kelly was quickly put onto a gurney, and before I knew what was happening they were wheeling her down the hall, cutting off her little outfit and sticking needles into her arm. I remembered I needed to call Carol back, but I didn't want to leave Kelly alone.

They must have given her Morphine Junior because soon Kelly was saying, "Papa, look at the butterflies." I knew it was okay to leave the room, so I went into the hall and called home.

"Carol, I really think you should come right away, her arm looks really bad." Carol hung up and quickly called a sitter to come stay with Mareah. Carol arrived on time to look at the x-rays with me—though we hardly needed verification of her compound fracture; the bone had come all the way through the skin.

The doctor walked over and introduced himself. He explained to us that Kelly needed to have some work done on her arm. He told us that they needed to go in, clean the gravel and dirt out of the hole, and then set the bones back into place. I felt light-headed. The knot in my stomach tightened. I looked over at Carol, and calmed down a little. It was as if God was gently saying to me, "Brett, trust me."

"Do what you need to do," I told the doctor.

Then the waiting began. The pacing and the waiting. Every time a doctor would come into the waiting room I would think it was for us, and when it wasn't I would go back to the pacing and waiting.

Finally Kelly's doctor came in and said, "Mr. and Mrs. Ray?"

I held my breath.

"Your daughter is just fine. Everything turned out great. When Kelly woke up she was quite excited."

"About what?" we asked.

"When she woke up, she realized she was wearing a hot pink cast and she is rather excited to show it off."

I exhaled.

Carol stayed with Kelly that night in the hospital because they were concerned about infection. Mareah stayed with Grammy and Bubba (my parents), and I took my three boys to visit Kelly the next morning. Kelly was excited to have company, and her brothers thought her cast was pretty cool.

"We're going to check out of here soon. Why don't you guys head out, and we'll meet you at home." Carol said. I really was trying to trust God with our little accident. It felt good to have the worst of it over.

The Trip Home

I must have passed the first test, because the second test came on fast and strong. On our way home from the hospital I was talking with the boys and I never saw him coming. We were hit by a car so hard that I got a mild concussion and bruised ribs; the other guy put his hand through the windshield.

The cars were slowly crawling by, holding up Carol who was just a short distance behind us. "Look, there's been an accident," she told Kelly. As she got closer she realized it was her husband and boys in the middle of the wreckage.

I know that broken bones and car accidents are not major life crises, but sometimes these little accidents in life can be a challenge for me. It's during these times that God whispers to me, "Brett, I want you to trust me—not just when life is going good, but when the tough times come along as well."

Over the years I have become well-acquainted with difficult times. One tragedy after another struck our family. My uncle fell off his tractor, was run over by the combine, and died. Another uncle was murdered while he was out celebrating a basketball victory with his buddies—shot over a traffic dispute. My dad's uncle was in a skydiving competition when his parachute did not open, and he was killed in front of his family. My aunt choked to death on a piece of steak in her apartment; she lived alone and she lay there for three days before the police broke in. Car accidents, cancer, and other illnesses have taken our loved ones.

When my cousin Mike was killed in a car accident, my Aunt Sandra, at the funeral, embraced the driver who was responsible for Mike's death, showing him that he was forgiven.

The man wept on my aunt's shoulder. This was a profound example to me of my aunt trusting God with a deep and painful wound that could have caused permanent resentment and bitterness.

When we go through tough times, we either draw closer to God or we push him away. We either trust him or we take matters into our own hands. Perhaps we start by asking why—but, if we trust him, eventually we realize that God is in control, even when we don't understand.

Getting Out of the Boat

Asking God "why?" is an age-old question. The disciple Peter (called Simon) seemed to ask God, "Why me?" when he was first called to be a follower of Christ and put his trust in Jesus. Jesus was teaching next to Lake Gennesaret (also called the Sea of Galilee). As usual, the people were crowding around Jesus. I can imagine Jesus' sandals getting wet as the crowds slowly pushed him into the water. I can see Jesus turning around and spotting a couple of boats behind him. *If I could just get into one of those boats,* he might have been thinking, *things would be much better. I could see the crowd better; they could hear me better.* "Hey," Jesus calls out to Simon, "would you mind if I got into your boat?"

Simon can't be a happy camper. He has been out all night fishing and has caught nothing. Zip. Fishing for fun was not what

Simon was doing. Fishing was his livelihood, his profession. He's probably done this his whole life. It's probably what his father and grandfather did. And now he's likely smarting from this flopped business venture. He's probably not in a very good mood—and Jesus comes walking up, smiles, and says, "Mind if I get in?"

Can you see the look on Simon's face as he's washing the nets with his blistered fingers, getting ready for his next trip out? "Yeah, fine, just don't touch anything. This equipment isn't cheap. Why don't you just sit over there and do your thing."

Jesus takes a seat and begins to teach. After a few stories, maybe a slight smile creeps over Simon's face. *This guy's good. My brother Andrew was right—this guy is really good.* You've just got to know that Jesus was probably the greatest storyteller these folks had ever heard.

Jesus finally finishes. Perhaps Simon had finished with his nets as well, and has been sitting quietly looking at the back of Jesus' head. Jesus spins around, and to Simon's surprise says, "Hey, Simon, let's go fishing."

Simon's thoughts begin to reel (no pun intended). "Fishing? Right, well, fishing's probably not going to work out right now. First, we just got the nets cleaned, stretched, and folded; second, we've been out all night long and have caught nothing. What I'm saying is, there're no fish out there. Maybe some other time."

I can see Jesus smiling, pausing, and replying, "Let's go anyway."

"Go anyway?" Simon responds, maybe a little irritated at this point. "Ok, maybe there's another way I can put this. The fish are on holiday. They've taken the day off and it would be a waste of your time, not to mention mine, to try to do any fishing right now."

Jesus smiles, pauses, and replies, "Let's go anyway. Come on, I'm kind of hungry; I haven't had any breakfast yet. It'll be fun."

Simon groans, "Yeah, sounds swell. Okay, look, because you ask, I'm going to do this."

I wonder if Simon's partners were exasperated: "You're not really going to do this! We just cleaned up."

Simon mumbles under his breath, "Look, maybe it will get him out of the boat. Let's just throw a net into the water."

They put out into the deep. I can see Simon throwing a net into the air as he thinks, *Let's teach the teacher by showing him that there are no fish out here in the daylight.* Simon sighs as the net hits the water and begins to sink. Suddenly, a tremendous yank makes those giant fisherman's muscles bulge. Simon's eyes widen as he looks down to see what looks like hundreds of fish. The nets begin to tear. Simon yells for his partners in the other boat, and they fill both boats so full that they begin to sink.

Can you see Jesus standing there with a grin on his face? I wonder if he was thinking, *I knew I created some fish over there a minute ago.* A miracle. Jesus of course knew it was a miracle. What I want to know is: how did Jesus do it? Did he just snap his fingers and the fish appeared or did he use some Aqua Man powers to signal the fish to swim in? I can see the dolphins out there saying, "Come on fish, get a move on it, we've got a miracle going on here."

Simon Peter had never seen anything like it; but he knew it was a miracle. No question, it was a miracle. He looks over at Jesus and says, in effect, "Get out of my boat!"

I can imagine Jesus' reply: "Is there something wrong? If you don't like flounder, I can do rainbow trout."

Simon says, "Look, it's not the fish, it's me. I'm a sinner and you're obviously something different than that. I would really appreciate it if you would just leave. It's been a rough day and I'm having a tough time with all of this."

Jesus steps out of the boat as he says, "Alright." But he turns around, reaching out his hand, looking Simon Peter in the eyes, and asking, "Simon, do you trust me?"

Simon looks down at the fish everywhere. "Do I what?"

"Do you trust me? Why don't you come out of the boat with me and I will make you a fisher of men." What Jesus was saying was, "Why not follow me and I will teach you how to fish for people. Why not trust in me and be a part of something eternal.

I know you're going through some tough times right now, but what a better time than this to invest your life in something that will last?"

A grin creeps over Simon's face. *I just told this guy that I'm a sinner and he still wants me to be one of his followers. Me? A disciple?*

The best part of the story isn't that the nets began to break or even that the boats began to sink. The best part of the story is that Simon got out of the boat. He left everything and put his trust in Jesus Christ. And though he made quite a few mistakes along the way, in the end, he trusted so deeply that he gave up his life and was killed for the man who taught him how to fish.

One of the Jesus movies that came out years ago shows Simon stepping out of the boat to follow Jesus. Before walking forward, Simon turns around, puts two hands on the boat, and pushes it out to sea. As he turns to follow Jesus, the camera pans out and you see the two men walking away while the boat is drifting out from the shore. That boat represents Simon's old life, his old way of doing things—of trusting in himself. Now he's pushing the boat away. Now he's putting his trust in the One who simply says, "Follow me."

Surrender

Jesus still has his hand outstretched and he's looking me in the eyes, asking if I will surrender, if I will follow, if I will trust him.

Are you trusting God through the tough times of your life? Maybe you're going through something you think God might consider small or trivial. God cares. He wants to be intimately involved in your life. He wants to be involved with every detail.

Maybe things have just been adding up over a period of time and you are feeling overwhelmed by life. God wants in. He loves you. Trust him by letting him have control over the minutes of your day. Sit down and surrender each thing to him. Place each one in his hands and let go of worry. When we worry, we are not trusting God. When we trust God we are not worrying.

Maybe you're going through something major right now. You're brokenhearted by the loss of a loved one. Or maybe you have been betrayed by someone you trusted. Or you have a relationship that is dear to you that is unraveling in front of your eyes. Whatever it is, climb out of the boat of self-reliance. Let God help you out of that boat and let him hold you. He is bigger than anything you are going through. Let him be God, and let yourself be the child who trusts him no matter what. He loves you and he understands exactly what you're going through. Climb out of the boat and put yourself, through prayer, into his hands.

Chapter Six

IN THE DARK

Fear

Roller Coaster Phobia

I grew up believing that carnival rides were made to hurt people. My family would go to the state fair and I would stand paralyzed in fear, tears rolling down my face, begging my mom not to let my fearless little brother ride the Ferris wheel. So, of course, my dad decided that our family reunions would be spent at an amusement park. From my childhood perspective, a trip to Boblo Island meant taking a boat to the park where you would be trapped all day on the island with creepy rides until the boat would pick you up at the end of the day. As I grew older, my cousins went on to bigger and better rides while I was still on the helicopters in Kiddy Land.

Then the dreaded year came when I was tall enough to go on any ride in the park. Peer pressure is a powerful thing.

Somehow my cousin, who is older than I am and much cooler, talked me into getting in line for the granddaddy of all rides in the park: the roller coaster. I got in line to impress him, but I couldn't hide the fact that I was terrified. The whole time I was in line, I kept hearing the "click, click, click, click, click" of the machine going up, followed by shrieks of terror as it went down. The whole time we were waiting I was saying, "You know these things aren't safe. You know we really shouldn't be in line for this thing. You know this really isn't a good idea."

After what felt like days of waiting, we finally reached the front of the line. We were next to get on—when something horrifying happened. The roller coaster flipped off the tracks right in front of our eyes. The sound of screeching metal and then an eerie silence fell over the onlookers. Something had jammed into the front wheel, causing the train to stop so abruptly that the back end flipped over, catapulting people out and onto the track. Nobody was killed, but people were obviously injured. A woman who had been thrown from the coaster stood up on the track, all blond hair and blood. I didn't realize she was in shock. I thought she was staring right at me and sending me a message: "Little boy, don't ride roller coasters."

I turned to my relatives, grabbed them, and said, "See, I told you so."

Pandemonium erupted through the crowd. People began screaming and pushing and running away as fast as they could from the nightmare in front of their eyes. We ran as well.

Later that day, my heart beating faster than it should, I stood staring at the coaster, which now looked like a scorpion with its tail bent over. It was still sitting silently in the same place I had last seen it. *I will never put my trust in one of these things again,* I silently vowed. *You will never catch me in line for another roller coaster.*

The years went by and I met and fell in love with Carol. I began to think, "What if when we get married, we have a houseful of children and they all love roller coasters? What if they want me to ride with them? I know they will still love me if I'm *Wimpy Dad,* but do I want to be *Wimpy Dad?*"

About two and half hours from my house, Cedar Point (the largest amusement park in the world) was building the tallest, fastest, steepest roller coaster in the universe—The Magnum XL 200. It would be the first roller coaster in the world to be built over two hundred feet high. I became consumed. If I was ever going to completely conquer my fear of roller coasters, I was going to have to trust God to help me ride the Magnum. I called my friend, John, and asked him if he would go with me to ride this beast. "I not only want to ride the Magnum the day it opens," I told him. "I want to be amongst the first riders to ever ride it."

John said, "Count me in."

My friends caught wind of our plan and began to send me information they could find on this coaster. Someone sent me a copy of an interview with the man who created the Magnum XL 200. I read it from start to finish, looking for those magical words: "Don't worry, it's safe." He never said that. Instead, he talked about how tall it was, how steep it was, how fast it was, and all the world records it was going to break. At the end of the interview he was asked if he was going to ride the Magnum. "No way," he answered promptly. "Do you think the guy who invented the electric chair wanted to try it out?"

Not to be deterred, John and I stayed in Sandusky, Ohio, the night before the park opened for the season. The next morning we were first in line for tickets. When the gates opened we ran as fast as our legs could carry us, with the great crowd of coaster enthusiasts running beside us. We got into the coaster, we buckled our seat belts, the train turned the corner, and we began our ascent. As I tightened my seat belt that brisk morning, two images flashed through my mind: the electric chair and a woman with blond hair saying, "Little boy, don't ride roller coasters."

We kept going up and up. Birds were flying underneath us. Airline pilots were waving at us and giving us the thumbs up. We finally reached the top. As I looked over the edge, up there on top of the world, I was tempted to close my eyes. I didn't. My white knuckles had a death grip on the bar as we raced down, over seventy miles per hour, and my breath was sucked out of my body. Up the next hill, through some fog-filled tunnels, screaming around corners, my body lifting from the seat as we hit the last hills—and then it was over.

I was alive. I jumped out of the train and raced down the exit ramp. Not caring who was looking, I let out a scream of victory as I jumped up and down and high fived my buddy John. People wanted to know what it was like. People may have been thinking that I was jumping and screaming because I had just conquered the tallest, fastest, steepest roller coaster in the world. But I was so excited because the little boy inside of me who had always been so afraid had, with God's help, defeated one of his deepest childhood fears.

True Fear

Overcoming the fear of roller coasters, I admit, is rather exhilarating. The story about my daughter's eyes was anything but fun.

I was having breakfast with the family, looking little Kelly in the eyes, when something happened that startled me. One of her eyes jumped. She was looking straight at me and one of her eyes bounced up and back down again.

"Did you see that?" I asked Carol.

"See what?"

"One of Kelly's eyes just jumped."

"It's still doing that?"

Shocked I said, "This has happened before?"

"Yes, it has happened a few times this week."

"Why didn't you tell me?"

"I was hoping it would just go away; but since it's not, I think we should take her to a specialist."

The doctor explained to us that he was going to have us put a patch over Kelly's good eye in hopes that it would straighten out the troubled eye. We asked, "What if it doesn't work?"

"Then we take the next step and put Kelly into glasses."

"What if the glasses don't work?"

"Then we'll have to talk about surgery, but let's cross that bridge if we have to."

So we put Kelly on the patch. (Sounds like our almost three year old was trying to quit smoking.) As the days went on, her eye seemed to be getting worse, so we took her back in. The doctor confirmed that her condition was getting worse and that she would need to start wearing glasses right away.

My family was joining me for my summer tour, and Kelly wore her little glasses the whole trip. She looked so adorable in her new frames; but by the end of summer, both eyes were now jumping around. As soon as the tour was over, we took her back in.

"I didn't catch it before," the doctor told us, "but it is now clear that Kelly has a rare eye disorder." He had seen it in only two other children in the last thirty-five years.

"So how do we treat it?" Carol asked.

"I'm sorry," he continued, "but she needs surgery. We'll have to put her under anesthesia for the surgery. I have an obligation to tell you that when a child is put under, there's always the slightest chance that they will never wake up again."

He started to tell us how remote the possibility was, but my head was dizzy anyway. *Never wake up?*

"Don't worry," he continued. "It has never happened to any of my patients, and I don't plan on Kelly being the first."

As is his way, God was whispering to my heart, "Brett, I want you to trust me. I want you to trust me with Kelly." I tried to comfort myself by believing that God would keep my baby safe; but then another whisper came: "I want you to trust me even if Kelly never wakes up again."

"Can we think about it?" I asked the doctor.

As the days went by, however, the decision to go ahead with the surgery became easier as Kelly would often wake up, lose her balance, and bump into walls.

On the day of Kelly's surgery, I woke up and told Carol I was doing well with our decision—and that I was going in with

Kelly. We had been told that only one parent could go in with her and hold her hand while they were putting her under.

"No way," Carol said. "I'm the nurse and you're a wimp. I'm going in because you'll freak out."

"Nope. I'll be fine. I've made up my mind."

"You'll regret it," she said.

We got to the hospital, and Kelly and I put on our scrubs. Despite that hospital smell that always makes me feel uneasy, I was doing fine—until we got into that cold surgical room. All of those strangers with masks over their faces, pointing to a cold table for me to lay Kelly on. I laid her down. She grabbed my hand tight and gave me a look that said, "Don't even think about leaving me in here."

She wasn't the only one afraid. I looked down and saw my hand trembling slightly. I started having second thoughts about them cutting my little girl's eyes and putting her under. What were the risks again? Losing her sight? Never waking up? I began to panic.

The doctor picked up a mask connected to the gas, looked at me and said, "This is going to smell like oranges, Dad."

I squeezed out the word, "Okay."

He said, "You need to tell Kelly."

Then I remembered I was supposed to be coaching my daughter. I bent over and whispered, "This mask is going to smell like oranges, Sweetie." But I didn't want that mask anywhere near Kelly's face. She squeezed my hand tighter.

I've changed my mind! I screamed silently.

The doctor put the mask over her face. Kelly's sweet little eyes rolled back and her hand that was squeezing mine so tight went limp.

I've changed my mind! Wake her back up! I wanted to shout, but I couldn't speak. My hands were shaking. The doctor sent the nurse over to my side of the table and she put her arm around mine.

"Mr. Ray, you're doing just fine." Then she began to pull me toward the door. I dropped Kelly's hand as the nurse said, "Your daughter is in good hands; everything's going to be okay." She pushed me out and shut the door and I could just picture her saying, "Wow, did they pick the wrong parent to do that or what?"

Then, to my absolute surprise, something happened that had not happened in years. I started to sob. I fell against the wall in the hallway. I burst into tears and cried and cried. I couldn't stop. I don't know how long I leaned there against the wall, but eventually I pushed myself up and started for the waiting room. I sat down next to Carol, who was reading a book. She looked over at me and said, "How did it go?"

I couldn't speak.

"Look at you," she said. "I told you this would happen." Then she got serious and said, "Brett, is Kelly okay?"

I nodded my head yes.

She said, "Are you okay?"

I nodded my head no.

The teasing stopped. "Come on," she said, "let's go to the cafeteria and get something to eat."

I have traveled for years sharing the message of hope that God can be trusted when we go through dark times. I'm the one who's always telling people to trust God and to know he's there for us no matter what we're going through. Now, I was in the dark once again—but this time more afraid than I had ever been. My prayer from the cafeteria was a desperate one, "God, please don't leave us. Please God, we need you right now, please don't forsake us."

The doctor finally came into the waiting room and said, "Kelly is waking up. You can come in now."

I looked over at Carol and asked her if I could hold Kelly first, and she graciously agreed. They brought Kelly to me and laid her in my arms. Almost right away, she tried to throw up. They told us this might happen. Nothing came out of her mouth, but as she strained, droplets of blood came out of her eyes and ran down her cheeks. I grabbed a cloth and began wiping the blood from her face.

My throat felt thick. I pulled Kelly closer to my chest. "I'll never let you go," I whispered in her ear. If someone had run up to our hospital room door at that moment and yelled, "Help! My family's trapped in our car, and it's on fire. Please, come quick!" I would have said, "I'm sorry, my precious daughter is bleeding out of her eyes and I wouldn't let go of her right now for anyone or anything. You'll have to go to the next room and see if there is someone there who can help you." This sounds extreme I know, but that's how I was feeling. Nothing could cause me to put that little girl down.

All of a sudden, I was consumed with this simple thought, *God the Father loves me.* An unusual time to be filled up with this simple truth, perhaps—while I'm wiping the blood from my daughter's face. But the enormity of his gift to me became suddenly evident. When his Son was bleeding from his head, blood dripping down his brow and through his eyes and onto his cheeks, God the Father set Jesus down to rescue me. When Jesus needed his Father the most, God turned his back and walked away to rescue me. Do you remember Jesus' words, "My God, my God. Why have you forsaken me?" Jesus knew the answer to his question. The car was on fire, I was trapped, and to rescue me, God set down his precious and only Son to rescue me from the flames. Jesus was forsaken, so I could be saved.

As I held Kelly in my arms, wiping the blood from her face, I thought, "I wouldn't have done it." I wouldn't set this little girl aside or sacrifice any of my children to save anyone. But, God the Father did. God the Father loves me. He is with me in the dark when I am so afraid.

The Storm

Jesus traveled from town to town teaching, preaching, healing and loving the people. One day, when it was time to leave Galilee and travel to the Gerasenes, the disciples and Jesus got into a boat to cross over the lake. I would be curious to hear the conversation between Jesus and his followers at this point.

"Jesus, you look exhausted. Why don't you pull up a cushion, lay down in the stern and sleep? Let us take care of the sailing. We know the waters well. Let us handle that. You get some rest."

I can hear Jesus saying something like, "Would you guys really do that for me? That would be great. Thank you so much."

They set out with Jesus asleep in the boat. A furious storm or squall comes up so suddenly that the waves are sweeping over the boat. The disciples think they are going to drown. For fishermen who probably lived on the waters their whole lives to be afraid says something about the magnitude of that storm.

I can just hear Peter yelling to the other guys between the explosions of thunder, "If we're going to die, we probably should wake up Jesus. He might want to know about it." Peter grasps Jesus' robe and shouts, "Jesus, wake up. We're going to die!"

Jesus has been sound asleep. Wiping the drool from his beard he yells back, "What? I can't hear you."

Peter's voice is trembling as he screams, "We're going to die! Don't you care?"

Jesus stands up, "What was that? With the wind and waves and all, I can't hear you."

Shouting once more, Peter cries, "Don't you care we're going to drown?"

Jesus shouts, "Hold on just a minute!" He turns around and yells to the weather, "Quiet! Be still!" Everything stops. Jesus turns back around and says, "Sorry about that. Now what were you saying?"

The men are frozen in terror. But, they're not sure what they are more afraid of: the storm that just vanished or the man who made it go away. Jesus, wiping the sleep out of his eyes, gets a little grin on his face. "What's the matter, fellas? You look a little pale."

The biblical account says that Jesus rebuked the wind and the raging storm and then asked the disciples, "Where is your faith?" The storm was raging, they were deathly afraid, and they forgot who was in the boat with them: the one who created the wind and the seas and their lives.

This is my problem. When the storms are raging, when I'm in the dark, when I am deathly afraid, I forget who is in the boat with me. Because I'm a child of God, Jesus will never leave me. He doesn't promise there will be no storms; but he does promise he will never leave us.

Do you forget who is in the boat with you? Do you, in the middle of your trials, try to survive on your own strength? Are you convinced that you are alone and that God is a million miles away and that he has forgotten you? Don't you know that he holds you in his arms when you sleep? "The Lord your God is with you. He is mighty to save. He will take great delight in you, he will quiet you with his love, he will rejoice over you with singing" (Zephaniah 3:17). "Never will I leave you; never will I forsake you" (Hebrews 13:5).

If you are a child of God, Jesus is in the boat with you. If you are not a follower of Jesus Christ, he wants to be in your boat. Isn't that what your heart cries out for—someone who will always be there for you? When you are afraid, you can trust God. If you have not been trusting him, he will forgive you and shower you with his grace. He chose to forsake his only Son to rescue you. He loves you.

Chapter Seven

COMMON THREADS

Family

About ten years ago I was speaking at a high school winter
ski retreat. I was taking turns riding the ski lift with different
teenagers to get to know them better. I was on my way up the slope
when I asked a student named Kelly a question that I have asked a
lot of students over the years. "How is your relationship with your
parents?" The most common responses are, "We fight a lot." "It's
okay, I guess." "I don't know my parents." "They don't understand
me." "We don't really get along." "I barely see them."

Kelly's response was quite different. "Oh, my parents,
they're my best friends."

Whenever I hear a teenager say something bizarre like,
"My siblings are my best friends" or "Mom and Dad? Yeah,
they're great" I have the urge to invite myself over for dinner and

ask mom and dad a million questions. "How did this happen?" "What did you do to make this come about?" "What are your secrets?" "Was it by accident?"

The dinners we've had with families across the country—with those who are friends with their family members—reveal common threads:

Embrace Imperfection

I was on another retreat, years ago, speaking to teenagers about God's grace and his forgiveness. It was a Saturday night and I challenged the students to confess their sins to Jesus and allow him to forgive them. Many of the leaders began praying with their students. Kids were teary-eyed as they opened up to God and each other. People were kneeling down next to their chairs and many of them had their arms around each other in prayer. It was a tender moment.

I stood on the stage, looking around the room to make sure that everyone who needed someone to pray with was being taken care of. I noticed a girl sitting on the stage to my left who was crying and had no one praying with her. I quickly looked around the room to see if any leaders were available to pray with her. Seeing none, I went over, sat down next to her, and asked, "Would you like me to pray with you?"

Tears streaming down her face, she said, "Yes! Please."

"How can I pray for you?"

She started to speak and then burst into tears again.

"It's okay," I told her. "Take your time. Share whenever you are ready." I have been speaking to students since 1986 and have heard a lot of horror stories come out of the mouths of teenagers. I had a feeling this was going to be another one of those moments. Whatever it was that was disturbing her to the point that she couldn't speak the words must be really bad. I waited.

Finally she stopped crying enough to say this to me. "I'm losing my..."

See, here it comes.

"I'm losing my.........4.0 grade average."

I paused. I wasn't sure if I could have heard her correctly. Very gingerly I asked, "What did you say?"

She looked exasperated, as if to say, "You're going to make me repeat it?" She said, "I'm getting a B+."

That's it? I wanted to laugh. Of course I couldn't laugh—this was obviously very serious to her—but you have to understand that I was kicked out of high school as a freshman. After I committed my life to Jesus and got back into school and passed my first class with a D-, my parent's threw a party. They brought out the fattened calf. "Our son passed a class!" A grade like that would be like gold to me. I wanted to say to this girl, "Take the B+ and run." But, of course, I couldn't do that.

Perhaps her parents were putting a lot of pressure on her. "What would mom and dad say if you brought home a B+?" I asked.

"They'd be thrilled."

"What?"

"Yes, they're always telling me to lighten up and to live a little. All I ever get are A's."

Okay, pressure's not coming from mom and dad. It must be from somewhere else.

"It's not just my grades I'm having trouble with," she offered. "It's also my car."

"What's wrong with your car?"

"Well, last year I got a new car. I have done a very good job of keeping it clean. It's just, lately, I have been too busy; now it's dirty and there's stuff on the floorboards. It's a mess."

Mess? I had three toddlers at the time. I figured this girl would be too shocked if I said something like, "You don't know what mess is until you get in my minivan. If I happen to get hungry while I'm driving I just scrounge around underneath one of the car seats to find some fries or gummy bears." I said nothing.

"It's not just my grades and my car, it's also my clothes."

"What's wrong with your clothes?"

"I try to keep them all color coordinated. The blue clothes are on blue hangers, the green clothes are on green hangers, the black clothes are on black hangers. But lately my closet is a disaster. I've got red clothes on yellow hangers."

Now I'm praying. *Lord, I don't know what to say to this girl. I just can't relate to her.* I keep all of my clothes in a big pile next to the bed. This drives my wife crazy. Carol asks, "Why do you have to keep all of your clothes in a pile next to the bed?"

I respond, "What if there's a fire in the middle of the night?"

She says, "But all your clothes?"

I say, "Well, you never know what kind of fire it might be."

I couldn't relate to this girl at all, so I didn't know how to pray for her. But then she said it: "And now you talk to me about having a personal relationship with Jesus Christ and it just doesn't work for me. I come on these retreats and I get all fired up about knowing God; then I go home and get in a fight with my mom—and my Christianity goes out the window."

That I could relate to. I remember going home after church retreats, so excited about what I learned from God and determined to pray every waking moment of the day, read my Bible without ceasing, and fast thirty days a month. Then, I would get home. Within hours I would have a fight with my mom or dad and would be up in my room crying, wondering where my Christianity had disappeared to. Why didn't Christianity work for me at home like it did at church?

As I sat there next to this young lady it occurred to me what her problem was. She was a perfectionist. If she couldn't get a 4.0 GPA, she felt like a failure. If her car was not in mint condition, she didn't even want to drive it. If her clothes were not properly organized, she didn't think she deserved them. If she couldn't have a perfect relationship with Jesus, she didn't believe it was real.

I looked at the young, tearful girl sitting next to me and I understood. If she can't have a perfect relationship with God, does she want to bother at all?

"There's no such thing as a perfect Christian," I told her softly.

She looked up, and I saw how desperately she wanted to believe that.

"The work that God has done in us through the life, death, and resurrection of Jesus Christ to save us from death is a perfect work. However, we are still stuck in these earthly bodies that will not be perfect until we see Jesus face to face in Heaven. We will fail, at times. That's why God gives us his grace. When God looks at us, he does not see our imperfections. He sees his Son, Jesus, who is perfect, whose Spirit lives in us." I squeezed her hand. "We're not perfect, and that's okay."

After we prayed together, I could see that a weight was lifted off her shoulders.

The apostle Paul admits that he is not perfect. "Not that I have already obtained all this, or have already been made perfect" (Philippians 3:12). Paul confesses that he has not obtained a lifestyle of purely walking by faith. He hasn't arrived yet. If a guy who wrote almost half of the books in the New Testament isn't perfect and that's okay, there's hope for me.

The perfect husband does not exist. There is no such thing as a perfect wife or perfect children. That's why we must rely on grace and forgiveness. This is a practice that I see among families who have healthy relationships—they trust in God's unconditional love with each other.

A lot of parents deal with fighting between their children by sending them to their individual rooms without any conflict resolution. When our children fight, they are not allowed to separate until they both sit down on the couch (preferably the love seat) and work things out. One of the children must look the other in the eyes and confess his or her offense. "I was wrong and I apologize for what I did." The other child must then forgive. "I forgive you for what you did." They can't leave until they have sincerely done this.

This rule stands for everyone in our family. Several years ago, my son Stephen, one of the twins, came up to me and said, "Papa, the way you talked to Momma a few minutes ago in the kitchen wasn't very nice."

Come here little man and I'll show you not nice. I didn't say that, but I sure thought it. However he wasn't being disrespectful; he was just modeling for me what I had taught him.

He took me by the hand and said, "Let's go apologize to Momma."

We walked to the doorway of the bedroom. Carol was working at her computer. I said, "Stephen here believes that I owe you an apology."

She looked at me and said dryly, "Stephen's a very smart kid."

"Carol," I said, "the way I talked to you in the kitchen a few minutes ago was wrong. Please forgive me."

Carol was grinning from ear to ear.

Why is she grinning? She's ticked off at me. Then I looked down at Stephen and he had this great smile on his face. His smile was saying, "Yep, my dad has to do this, too." Grace at work in our imperfect home. Relying on grace and forgiveness is one of the ways we trust God with our families.

Let Go of the Past

When I got married I had an anger issue and didn't realize it. One month after the honeymoon, I was in the kitchen of our new apartment, raising my voice at Carol, gritting my teeth and getting right in her face. I took a step back and thought, *Wow, where did that come from?* Carol was probably thinking, "Who is this stranger that I married?"

I knew I was an angry teenager, but I didn't realize until then that I was an angry adult. I had an anger problem.

I guess I could have used Paul's words in Philippians 3:12 to justify telling Carol that "I'm not perfect and this is what you're stuck with." However, in 3:13 he says that we need to put the past behind us and strain toward what is ahead. I knew what I needed to do, but I couldn't do it alone. To put my anger in the past and to strain toward what was ahead, I needed help.

I called my pastor and confessed my anger problem to him. I talked to one of my best friends, told him about my problem, and said, "Every time I lose my temper, you're going to hear about it and you're going to pray with me." I also got some wise counsel on anger management. Today, my wife will tell you that she is married to a different person than the man she married in 1989. God gave me the strength and help to put my anger problem in the past.

We need to put the past behind us and strain toward what is ahead. We need to deal with the issues in our lives and build relationships that are growing forward and not slipping backward. However, putting the past behind us and straining toward what is ahead is easier said than done. There are two things that have helped me a great deal in this area. The first is setting goals before God and the second is having accountability for those goals.

Setting Goals

Let me share with you a few of the goals I have set over the years regarding my family and my friendship with God. The three most important relationships in my life are: my relationship with God, my relationship with my wife, my relationship with my children, in that order of importance. Let's look at one goal I have set for each of these three relationships.

My relationship with my children: I came up with something years ago called "Papa Time"—one-on-one time with each of my children. When the kids were younger, they would fight over whose turn it was for Papa Time. Why? Because they crave spending time with their dad. We do it in birth order so that I can remember whose turn it is.

Here's how it works: Rather than running to the store alone, I'll take one of the kids. "Okay, whose turn is it for Papa Time?" I'll ask. Kelly will put on her coat and strut out to the car as if to say, "Yeah, it's my turn."

On the way to wherever it is we're going, I do my best to get into their lives. "So, Kelly, what's your favorite part of school?"

"My favorite part of school is art because we are making these beautiful flowers."

Of course, it is something completely different if I ask the boys. "The best part of school is gym because we were playing this game where you cream the other guy with a ball." There is a difference between boys and girls. My daughters play with dolls; my boys try to invent ways to blow up the dolls with their battlefield toys. Papa Time has just been one way to tell my kids that they are a priority in my life.

My relationship with my wife: Back in 1988, Carol and I went to pre-marriage counseling. "After you marry Carol," the pastor told me, "don't stop dating." I took his words seriously and set a goal to take my wife on a date at least once a week. We can probably count on two hands how many dates we have missed since September 1989. Dating is no longer a goal; now it's a part of life. We have it in the budget, it's a night we look forward to, and it's been great for our marriage. Date night has been a way for me to say, "You are a priority to me."

My relationship with God: A half hour of focused time with the kids is good. A regular date night with Carol is good. However, I can imagine God saying, "What I want is a whole day. Every week." God was serious enough about this that he put it in the Ten Commandments. Set aside one day to be sacred, to be holy, to be special. Don't forget to have a Sabbath.

At our house we call our Sabbath "Yea God Day." It is our family's favorite day of the week. We often start off with "Circle

Time." Our kids love Circle Time because we sing worship songs together as a family. Most of us can't carry a tune, but that doesn't stop us. Throughout the day we do things the kids look forward to—things like flying kites, launching rockets, renting movies, riding bikes, inviting friends over, or going out for dinner. Carol doesn't cook on our Sabbath, I don't do any public speaking, and the kids don't do any of their chores. It is a day set aside to celebrate God's presence in our lives.

Being Accountable

Setting goals is useless if I don't work to achieve those goals. I have met with a group of guys for years to have them hold me accountable for goals I have made. This has been life-changing for me. I have grown in my relationship with God and have grown as a husband and a father.

Setting goals and having accountability has helped me to put the past behind me and to strain toward what is ahead. God has helped me to overcome issues in my life and to strengthen relationships. Families that have healthy relationships are families who know the importance of putting the past behind them and straining toward what is ahead.

Persevere

Carol and I are best friends. I trust her and love her more than anyone else. However, if we had based our relationship with each other on our feelings, we would have been divorced a long time ago. Sometimes we just don't like each other. So what? Our relationship is based on a covenant that we made before God to stay together until death separates us, not until we get annoyed with each other. Sometimes we just have to press on.

It was about 3:00 a.m. Carol jumped out of bed into the dark. She elbowed me accidentally on her way out and woke me up. I could tell she was in a panic. She ran toward the bathroom but stopped in the bedroom and got sick on the floor. She ran again toward the bathroom, but got sick in the hallway. She got sick again on the bathroom floor before making it to the toilet.

I laid in bed thinking a couple thoughts. *Pretend like you're sleeping, for crying out loud! Don't move a muscle or you're dead.* I coached myself. *She's a nurse. She's used to cleaning up messes. She'll do just fine.* Why would I think that? Because that is the kind of husband I naturally am. A selfish, self-centered husband who thinks only about himself. Do you know how I know there is a God? I reached over and turned on the light. Brett Ray without Jesus Christ in his life would have never turned on that light.

Against my will, I got up, walked into the bathroom, and turned on the lights. There was my beautiful bride, nine months pregnant, with intense food poisoning. She was a mess. I got down on my knees and slowly began to clean up. I started feeling a little nauseated myself. I looked over at her and said, "I love you."

"I know you do."

"Oh yeah, how do you know that?"

She said something to me that I'll never forget. "Because you love me even when you don't feel like it."

I wish that was always the case. A lot of the time I keep my eyes closed. I say, "It's not my problem." I do it with my kids too. Kids can drive anyone crazy with all their demands. But when we had them dedicated, we made a promise in front of our friends that we would train up our children in the way of the Lord. We didn't say we'd quit doing this when it got hard.

God has been our ultimate example of unconditional love. He doesn't give up on us. He is committed to loving his children forever. Jesus Christ is the one who loves us even if he doesn't feel like it. Jesus did not feel like dying on the cross. How many times did he pray in the garden for God not to let what was about to happen, happen? "Father, if you are willing, take this cup from me; yet not my will, but yours be done" (Luke 22:42). Jesus did not want to be separated from his father because of our sins. He was beaten until his flesh was in pieces and he was nailed to a tree. He submitted to his father's perfect will and showed his love for us by pressing on so that we could put our past behind us and have life eternal with him.

We are not perfect.

We can leave the past behind us.

We must press on.

Chapter Eight

SOUL MATES

Friendship

When I read the Bible, I like to be on the lookout for what I call gold nuggets. These nuggets can be a verse in the Bible that God uses to communicate truths that he wants me to apply to my life—not to say that the whole Bible doesn't need to be applied to my life, it's just that it's a big book and he tends to teach me a little at a time. A little known Bible story about Jonathan has offered up two wonderful nuggets about friendship.[1]

Heart and Soul

God's chosen people, the Israelites, had enemies. However, they were accustomed to winning battles in times of war because God's blessing was on them. But, in this particular story, the Israelites are not doing well. The Philistines have beaten them down so only the king and his son have weapons. The Israelites are hiding from the Philistines. Why are they losing so bad? Because King Saul has slowly been turning his heart away from God; God is no longer blessing the Israelites the way he has done in the past.

The story continues:

> Now a detachment of Philistines had gone out to the pass at Micmash. One day Jonathan son of Saul said to the young man bearing his armor, "Come, let's go over to the Philistine outpost on the other side." But he did not tell his father.
>
> —1 Samuel 13:23-14:1

Hiding out in caves and holes is not how God has given his chosen people victory in the past, and Jonathan is not going to sit around doing nothing. He and his armor bearer leave the protection of the Israelite army and go over to the enemy outpost to see if they can take on the Philistines.

Probably the best way to describe an armor bearer is to use a golfing term. An armor bearer was like a caddy. A caddy serves the golfer, carrying his clubs and making suggestions on which club is needed for specific situations during the match. In the same way, an armor bearer assisted the prince by carrying weapons and fighting alongside the prince in battle. A prince and his armor bearer would likely grow close to one another, fighting side by side through many battles and watching out for one another in life-threatening situations.

> Saul was staying on the outskirts of Gibeah under a
> pomegranate tree in Migron.
>
> —I Samuel 14:2a

Jonathan and his armor bearer are boldly striding into danger, and now the writer stops the action to tell us the king is standing under a pomegranate tree in Migron. Who cares? Let's get on with the story.

> With him were about six hundred men,
> among whom was Ahijah, who was wearing an
> ephod. He was a son of Ichabod's brother Ahitub
> son of Phinehas, the son of Eli, the LORD's priest
> in Shiloh.
>
> —I Samuel 14:2b-3a

Again, the writer is stalling Jonathan's heroic action with boring details. Is there a reason for talking about a pomegranate tree and ephods (whatever an ephod is)? Yes, the writer is taking time out to tell us the King and his priest who wore the ephod (who should be claiming a victory for God) are holding court in the comfortable shade of a tree.

> No one was aware that Jonathan had left.
>
> — 1 Samuel 14:3b

Not only did the king not know that Jonathan had left, but no one did! No back up for Jonathan and his armor bearer if things go bad. Apparently Jonathan was more passionate about his purpose than his safety.

> On each side of the pass that Jonathan
> intended to cross to reach the Philistine outpost was
> a cliff; one was called Bozez, and the other Seneh.
> One cliff stood to the north toward Micmash, the
> other to the south toward Geba.
>
> —1 Samuel 14:4-5

Okay, what's with the geography lesson? Well, the writer is telling us now that the route that Jonathan and his armor bearer were taking was a valley that passed between two cliffs. Because the Philistines were up on top of those cliffs, this was going to be very dangerous and Jonathan would now be a very easy target.

> Jonathan said to his young armor-bearer,
> "Come, let's go over to the outpost of those
> uncircumcised fellows. Perhaps the LORD will act
> in our behalf. Nothing can hinder the LORD from
> saving, whether by many or by few."
>
> —1 Samuel 14:6

Notice the word "perhaps." This is where it gets almost humorous. What would you say if you were the armor bearer? "Let me get this straight. We are leaving the rest of the army behind. Just the two of us are going to take on the enemy. We have told no one what we're doing. We are walking between two cliffs. We have one weapon between the two of us and now you're saying, 'perhaps God is going to show up.'" If I'm the armor bearer, I'm saying I need more than just a "perhaps." I want a "definitely, no doubt about it, God is absolutely going to show up" if I'm going through with this. But that's not what the armor bearer says.

> "Do all that you have in mind," his armor-
> bearer said. "Go ahead; I am with you heart and
> soul."
>
> —I Samuel 14:7

Gold nugget number one: choose friends who support your God-given dreams with their heart and soul.

I am a weak person. I've always needed help. I do not want to try to win this race or this battle called life alone. So I have surrounded myself with men who love God, who will run this race with me—godly men who will fight alongside of me. I thank God that he has brought these men into my life, friends who are with me heart and soul. They encourage me, strengthen me, and help me grow closer to God. They challenge me to be a better husband, a better father; they hold me accountable to run the race in such a way as to get the prize.

Do you have a friend like that?

Walk Your Talk

Jonathan said, "Come, then; we will cross over toward the men and let them see us. If they say to us, 'Wait there until we come to you,' we will stay where we are and not go up to them. But if they say, 'Come up to us,' we will climb up, because that will be our sign that the LORD has given them into our hands."

—1 Samuel 14:8-10

Jonathan didn't know for sure what was going to happen, but he was willing to risk his life for God all the same.

So both of them showed themselves to the
Philistine outpost.

—1 Samuel 14:11a

How exactly did they show themselves? I can't wait to get
to heaven and see the replay on that one.

"Look!" said the Philistines. "The Hebrews
are crawling out of the holes they were hiding in."
The men of the outpost shouted to Jonathan and his
armor-bearer, "Come up to us and we'll teach you a
lesson."
So Jonathan said to his armor-bearer, "Climb up
after me; the LORD has given them into the hand of
Israel."

—1 Samuel 14:11b-12

Look at this next part:

Jonathan climbed up, using his hands and
feet...

—1 Samuel 14:13a

"Using his hands and feet" suggests that he was climbing
up a steep cliff. This probably put them in a vulnerable situation.

> …with his armor bearer right behind him.
>
> —1 Samuel 14:13b

Gold nugget number two: choose friends who put their words into action.

The young man who was Jonathan's armor bearer was not all talk and no walk. He told Jonathan that he was with him heart and soul, and then he followed through by climbing up the cliff himself, using his hands and feet.

At times, people have said to me, in one way or another, "I am with you heart and soul" without following through. They bailed out.

Do you have friends who are right behind you? When you turn around, they are climbing up after you, rooting you on?

Soul Mates

I won't tell you what happened to Jonathan and his armor bearer. It really doesn't matter much, for our purposes. What is important is that they were willing to give their lives for each other—and much more importantly for God. (I have to admit: the end of the story is a good one. You can read about it in 1 Samuel 14:14-23.)

Carol and I are grateful for the true friends we have. We pray that our children will grow up having friends who are with them heart and soul and who are right behind them—friends who will encourage them to know God in a greater way.

If you don't have a friend like that, pray that God will bring someone into your life who will strengthen, encourage, and help you to grow.

Jesus, ultimately, is your best friend. He cares so much about you and he loves you. Jesus Christ is the ultimate armor bearer. He climbed up a mountain on his hands and feet, carrying a cross on his back for you. He died, rose again, and is alive today. He has already won the battle for you. He is with you heart and soul.

1. This passage and the comments here were pointed out to me years ago by one of my friends, who was also a travel companion and one of my teachers. This chapter was inspired by him. Thank you Rick.

Chapter Nine

TAKING A STAND

Eternity

I was walking out the door with my family, on our way to church, when two kids from the neighborhood got in the face of my oldest son. Josh was about six years old. As I was walking by I heard one of the boys say, "We've decided that we like you, but not your twin brothers. They're just little kids. If you want to hang around us anymore, you've got to lose them."

Josh took a step back and said, "Well, if you don't want to be their friends, I guess I won't hang around you. I'm sticking with them."

"Well, then you're a baby!"

"Yeah," the other kid said, "you're nothing."

Josh shrugged his shoulders and walked away. I glanced over at my wife while we were loading the other kids into the van.

I gave her a look that said, "Did you catch that?" We drove off, and Joshua burst into tears. I pulled the van over, picked him up out of his seat and sat him on my lap. Wiping the tears from his face I asked, "Josh, what's wrong?"

Through his tears he said, "Papa, I lost my friends."

"No, Josh," I said, "you kept your friends and in the process you became a hero."

He looked at me with a puzzled look on his face and said, "What do you mean?"

"Josh, your brothers are your real friends and now you are their hero for sticking up for them." Smiles appeared on the faces of Stephen and Andrew. I said, "Josh, true friends would not ask you to do what those two kids just asked you to do. You made the right choice by standing up for your brothers and I'm proud of you. You're a hero, Josh!"

Josh grinned.

How far did Josh go? How far does love go? Josh was willing to take a stand for what was right. In that moment, Josh took a stand for something that could last forever, his friendship with his brothers. That night at church, Josh brought his Bible memory verse home on a piece of paper. It simply said, "A friend loves at all times." We felt God gave that verse to Josh as a special gift that night.

The Choice

If I had asked Josh why he chose his brothers over his friends, he would have simply replied, "Because they're my brothers." This may seem the obvious choice and yet making the obvious choice is sometimes hard. God is the best friend we could ever hope to have; yet we are often ashamed to claim his friendship in front of others.

I was on a flight from Detroit to Atlanta, on my way to speak at a marriage conference, and I had all my notes on my lap. About an hour into the flight, the woman sitting next to me spoke up for the first time, "Excuse me, sir, could I ask you a question?"

"Okay," I said.

"I hope you don't mind, but I have been looking over your shoulder at your notes and I was just wondering, is this marriage conference material?"

"Yes, it is,"

"So, are you a marriage conference speaker?"

"Yes, I am."

Very timidly she asked, "Could I ask you something?"

Once again, I said "Okay," not sure where this was going.

"My divorce was final a few months ago and I was just wondering, when will the pain go away?" Her question was not the slightest bit vindictive and she was being very sincere, speaking from a broken heart.

What an opportunity to brag about my Friend who is the great Healer. But I was afraid. The only hope I had to give this woman came from my having a relationship with Jesus Christ. But I was tempted to keep him to myself. This was an opportunity to gently take a stand for Christ and not be ashamed of him.

In the moment it took for me to open my mouth, I gave myself an extensive lecture. *What are you waiting for, Brett? Will you surrender to fear, settle into your comfort zone—or will you live for something greater, deeper, and lasting? If you're living for eternity, then what matters is that which is lasting. Your fear is here for a moment; God's love is here forever. This woman's eternity could be impacted! A woman without hope could be led to the Giver of Hope.*

"I wish I had a pill to give you that would make all your pain go away," I said. "I wish I had something magical to say to you that could heal your broken heart. But, the only thing I know of that can begin to touch your pain is a personal relationship with Jesus Christ. He understands what's going on in your heart and he loves you. He can walk you through this hurt and be there with you."

She looked away.

"Can I ask you a question?" I asked.

Her answer was noncommittal. "Okay."

I took another deep breath, another lecture to myself blaring in my mind. I asked, "Could I pray with you?"

"Right here?"

"Yes."

"Right now?"

"Yes."

She looked at me like I had just asked her to jump out of the plane without a parachute.

"I guess."

"Okay, let's pray." I took her by the hand and we bowed our heads. I prayed a very simple prayer—that God would meet her right where she was, that she would let God begin to touch those broken places inside of her. Something happened while we were praying. First she began to tremble. I looked up, continuing to pray. She had her head still bowed, but tears began to stream down her face. Then she began to sob. I finished praying.

She squeezed my hand and said, "I had no idea how much I needed that." It made me think what she was getting at was how much she needed him. Then she wouldn't stop talking to me for the rest of the flight. That was just fine with me.

Once again, I almost let fear rule the day. I almost didn't say anything about where my hope comes from. I almost didn't stand. God will give us the strength every time when we need it— if we will lean on him, live for him, and keep eternity in our minds and hearts. God's love lasts forever. "I am not ashamed of the gospel, because it is the power of God for the salvation of

everyone who believes: first for the Jew, then for the Gentile"
(Romans 1:16).

Through the Roof

Do you know the story of the four men who helped their
friend to stand? As was the case so often when Jesus was teaching,
the crowds were pressing in on him; on this day, the house Jesus
was in was packed, with people crowded even outside the door.
These four men believed if they could just get their friend, who
could not walk, to Jesus, he would heal him. But they could not get
in. They couldn't even get close.

How far would they go? How far does love go? "Jesus is
the healer, and we will get him to Jesus how ever we can," they
said. The crowds didn't stop them, the opinions of others didn't
stop them. They headed up to the roof. I picture Jesus standing
there, sharing a parable. He spits dust out of his mouth that fell on
him from above. He pauses, and then continues. A minute later he
is spitting and squinting his eyes. The dust and dirt are now falling
freely onto his head and into his eyes and mouth. He looks up and
lets out a little laugh as he sees a hole—a rather large hole—
appearing through the ceiling above him. The crowds begin to
laugh. The owner of the house is not laughing. Jesus whispers to
the owner, "I know a little about carpentry. I'll take a look at it
later."

Jesus can now see the sky and the dirty faces of four determined heroes. "Hello, up there. What can I do for you?"

"Glad you asked," one of the men shouts down. "We have a friend we want you to meet." The four men lower their friend down on a mat, right in front of Jesus.

Jesus heals the man's legs—but better than that, he heals the man's heart. "Son, your sins are forgiven. Get up, take your mat and walk."

The man stands. He walks out of the house in full view of everyone, and they praise God saying, "We have never seen anything like this!"

The four men took a stand—motivated by their love for their friend—and now their previously crippled companion is standing. Jesus Christ gives us the strength and the courage to stand, and amazing things happen.

I Am Not Ashamed

We were in a fast food restaurant once and it had one of those play lands. You know, the claustrophobia tubes that the kids love to crawl through. Before my kids are allowed to go up, climb, play, and slide, they get the same little speech from me every time there are other kids around. My kids know what's coming. As they're taking off their shoes I say, "Okay guys, I want you to look out for the other kids up there. I don't want you to push other kids out of your way. I don't want anyone sliding down on somebody else's face, and if there's a kid up there who's scared, help him find his way down. Okay, go have fun." Same speech. Every time.

On this particular day, quite a few other parents were present and I noticed they were listening to my little list of rules. If I could guess, I would say they were thinking, "Hey, I like this. This guy's kids are going to be looking out for mine." I looked over and smiled. They smiled back.

A couple of minutes went by when one of my twins spoke up loud enough for us to hear him up there. We couldn't see him, but we could hear him. "Hi," he said. "I'm Andrew."

The other kid said, "Hi, I'm Billy."

And then very loudly Andrew said, "Billy, do you know Jesus?"

I felt the eyes of every parent sitting around me turn on me like laser beams. It was as if they were now saying, "Oh, we've got your number, *Jesus Freak*." A rush of embarrassment ran through my blood before I could catch myself. Or, more accurately, before God could catch me. "Hey, Brett," he whispered to me. "See that? See Andrew? That's what I want from you. See how he's not ashamed of me? See how he hasn't learned how to doubt me yet? Andrew is not afraid to take a stand for me."

I leaned back and smiled. *Go, Andrew.*

God has given me a purpose in my life, to live for him. He has given me hope—hope that there is more to this life than the here and now, hope that will carry me into the future. He has died in my place on the cross. He rose from the dead and is not ashamed to tell me today, "Brett Ray, I love you."

Isn't it time for me to get over my embarrassment? Isn't it time for me to get over myself? Isn't it time for me to trust God? Isn't it time to take a stand?

Chapter Ten

LEAP OF FAITH

Conclusion

During the summer months, my family comes with me as I travel from camp to camp. Several years ago, when Kelly was four, we arrived at a camp in South Carolina to find out they had a zipline. If you don't know what a zipline is, count your blessings. It is a steel cable extending from point A to point B, with the sole purpose of flinging a human being at sickening speeds across its length. At this particular camp, the suicidal person has to climb onto a platform up in the trees to reach point A. Point B was on the other side of the lake. This person puts on a body harness which connects to a sliding device (a trolley) that attaches to the cable. Locked onto the cable, she takes a leap of faith off the platform (which, let me remind you, is miles up in the air) and zips, as my boys would say, one hundred thousand miles per hour across the lake. To slow down, she splashes into the water, skids across the surface of the lake, and eventually stops. Some would consider it quite a thrill ride.

Right away my three boys began begging me to let them go on it.

"Knock yourself out," I told them.

As they ran off to conquer the zipline, I asked my daughter, Kelly, if she wanted to watch. She was excited to do that. A dock that you could walk to was strategically placed in the middle of the lake for optimum viewing, so Kelly and I sat down where we had front row seats. We watched the people jumping off, zipping past, and then splashing down. My oldest son, Josh, was locked in and ready to go. He took the leap of faith, yelling out at the top of his lungs. He zipped past us, and then with a mighty splash, hit the water. I looked over at Kelly and said, "Wow, did you see that?!"

"Yeah!" she breathed.

"That was incredible!"

"Yeah!"

"Would you like to try it?"

"NO!" With a very serious look on her face she exclaimed, "Papa, don't tease me. I'm too small."

"I bet they would let you try it."

Once again, very seriously, she said, "Stop teasing me."

"Okay."

We then watched Stephen, one of the twins, jump. At least I think it was Stephen. ZIP! SPLASH! And then his twin brother. ZIP! SPLASH!

Kelly looked up at me, and with a frightened look, said, "Papa, if you go up there with me, I'll jump."

I was surprised, but proud. "That's my girl," I said. "Let's go!" I raced her over to the zipline before she had time to change her mind. I looked at the man in charge and said, "Hey, do you have a harness her size?"

He looked at little Kelly and said, "Yes, we can hook her up."

We climbed to the top and locked Kelly's harness onto the zipline. I was getting nervous, but I wanted to see her conquer her fear.

The hardest part of the zipline is, of course, the jump. You are trusting that this line is going to catch you as you take the leap of faith. I was so proud of Kelly for just getting up there that I decided to take the greatest element of fear (the jump) out of the equation. My plan was to lift Kelly up, lean out, and gently set her on the line so she could start off nice and slow and then gently gain momentum.

I looked down at Kelly and said, "Are you ready?"

She looked back at me and said, "Yes." Before I could grab onto her to lift her up, she leapt off of the platform and into the air.

"KEEELLLYY!!!" I screamed.

She sailed over the lake and splashed down. A hush fell over the crowd as they waited to see what Kelly's response would be. Kelly stood up in the water and said, "I...I...I want...I want to do it again."

Everyone began to cheer. I shouted, "Way to go, Kelly!"

That night, as I was heading up to the auditorium to speak to the students, the youth pastor stopped me and said, "I saw your daughter jump today."

I said, "Oh, yeah. I'm proud of her."

"I'm sure you are; but you missed the best part."

"What do you mean?"

"When Kelly jumped today, you were behind her and you missed it."

"What did I miss?"

"I was on the dock and I could clearly see her face. When she jumped off that platform she had one look written all over her face."

"Tell me."

"The look said one thing: 'I trust my dad.'"

That's what God wants from me. He wants the look written all over my face to say, 'I trust my Dad.'"

We have a heavenly daddy who wants us to trust him. Our heavenly Father wants so badly for us to believe in him with everything we have and with all of who we are. He wants us to trust him through the good and bad times. He wants us to trust him with our relationships. He wants us to trust him with our futures. He wants us to trust him with our lives. He wants us to trust him with everything.

Life sometimes feels like a leap of faith. It's worth it. God is with you, always there to hold you up. He loves you. He is crazy about you. People may let you down; life may let you down. But God has a perfect track record. He has always been there for you.

Life is short. Trust God today with your life and your future. Don't wait until it's too late. Put your faith in him. Move beyond your doubt and believe.